Cover art by Colleen Ingram

ISBN- 13: 978-149-2235484

ISBN -10: 1492235482

Registration Number: TXu001646678

Make Love Enough

by

Arthinia Morgan

·

Chapter 1
This Is Your Life

Michelle

I have had enough! Every time I turn around somebody needs something. Gayle needs advice on her *no good* husband, Marie needs help finding and keeping a man, and Faye needs advice on life all the way around. On top of that, I have a husband, three kids, a house and a dog to take care of. Not to mention a job that drives me crazy and a family that is running a close second to the job. I mean, cut a sista a break please. For someone who seems to always have it together, I feel like I am coming apart at the seams.

I have been married for fifteen years. We have one daughter and two sons. This morning I realized that I spend a total of fifteen minutes alone a day. My mornings are spent rushing to get the kids ready and off to school, then rushing to get to work, then rushing to pick the kids up, then rushing home in the evenings. My weekends are spent doing household chores, playing chauffer to the kids, going to the hairdressers and then Sunday we're off to church. Then back home for a good ol' home cooked Sunday dinner and then I'm off and running getting everyone ready for the week. I know, I know what you are thinking; this is a typical day for a mom. But I'm drowning yall. I live for the day when my sweet husband and I can sleep until at least ten and cuddle and do forbidden things all day long. Don't get me wrong, I love my babies; I just want them to go away sometimes. Is that so wrong?

Faye

Today I spent the entire day with my ear glued to the phone.
Michelle is helping me "discover" myself, again. Today I want to
open a unisex hair salon. Yesterday it was a shelter for
misunderstood Dalmatians and last week it was a Soul Food
restaurant. I am a master chef in my own right. Shucks, I've been
cooking since I was twelve. Can I help it if I have a generous heart?
Since college my girls have always been there to help me make life's
decisions. Gayle and Marie won't say it, but I know they think I'm a
lost cause. Michelle is the only one that ever listens. I'm thirty-one
years old and I have no clue as to what I want to do with the rest of
my life. My boyfriend of eight months just moved out. Did I
mention that it was while I was at work and that he took all of my
furniture and my darn $400 cookware? I really thought he was the
one.

When will I ever learn, just 'cause he can make you feel good in bed,
doesn't mean he's marriage material. Oh well, back to the drawing
board. Maybe, if my big headed boss would stop micro-managing
me I could search for my true path in life. Instead I'm stuck
balancing books and reconfiguring revenue for an advertising and
marketing firm. Yes it's a six figure income but it isn't my true
passion. Now, if I could just figure out what my true passion is....

Gayle

That bastard, I know he's cheating. No man has that many female
friends and isn't screwing at least one of them. And why does he
need two cell phones? And what are all of these mysterious
purchases on the Visa bill? And what the hell is he doing on the
internet at one in the morning when he's got all of *this* in bed waiting
on him? Every time I come close to catching him, that smooth talker
distracts me with his beautiful, long, rock hard member and I second
guess myself. Well not this time. I guess I've always known he was
no good. I think it was the chase that made me want him so darn

4

bad. He had an ass so tight you could open a cola with it. Tall and so dark he disappeared at night. And when he touched me I'd forget my name for a minute. When I walked in on him and my *friend* two weeks before our wedding, you'd think reality would set in. Umph, I love that bastard.

Marie

So what if I'm a bit brusque at times. I've always been independent and strong willed. Insecure men hate that. I have my own business, an African-American book store called Amhara. My four bedroom house is bought, paid for and laid out I might add. My financial portfolio is superb. Why is it that every man I meet is intimidated by a self-made woman? I mean what? I'm in shape, I am gainfully employed, I go to church and I don't need him to take care of me. What more can a man want? I'm trying to give the brothers a chance but I'm seriously thinking about crossing over. I am thirty-three years old and my eggs are slowly drying up! Can I get someone to fertilize these things before it's too late? Michelle says that I shouldn't be afraid to let a man lead. Lead me to what, the poor house? WHATever! A sister is doing things for herself. Maybe I'll do the modern thing and get knocked up with a test tube. Shucks, we've been raising rug rats for years on our own. I don't need a man.

Chapter 2
Everything for Everybody

"Baby, dinner was delicious as usual," Anthony said as he wrapped his muscular arms around my waist. "Why thank you sweetie." I say as I playfully whack him with dish towel. His hands traveled slowly down my waist and he gently squeezed my ample bottom. "Watch out now, don't start nothing." I say turning away from the sink so that I could look him in the eye. Is it a sin for a man to feel so good? The kids were sitting at the dinner table and they all looked over at us. My youngest, Michael who's three said what the others were thinking, "What Mommy, don't start what?" Michelle blushed a little. "Nothing baby, Daddy's just being a bad boy." I said trying to wiggle from his grasp. Michael gave Anthony a disapproving look. "No snack for you, daddy" he said. "OK son," Anthony responded while winking at me. That was my cue to make sure that Jr., Alyssa, and Michael were in bed a little early tonight.

My husband, who by far is one of the best examples of a husband and dad by far, is so good to me. He's owned his own trucking business for ten years and provides very well for us. Gayle and Marie think I spoil him too much. *"Do you let the man use the bathroom by himself, Michelle," "Is the man capable of making his own plate, Michelle?"* they say. I have no problem reminding them, umm…hello, my man is good to me so I am good to him. Besides, what's wrong with a clean house and a wife making sure her man is satisfied? At 39, six foot two and 225 lbs, my man looks just as good as the day we met. If I won't do it, there's a wench waiting in the wings that will!

The phone rings and I'm praying it isn't Faye (my surrogate child) again. "Hello" I say putting the leftovers in the fridge. Anthony is looking at me and asking the silent question of who's on the phone.

6

I sigh and cradle the phone between my shoulder and my ear and push the start button on the dish washer. "Hey Faye, what's going on girl?" I say while walking into the family room. Anthony gives me a goofy look and the kids all yell, "hey Auntie Faye" in unison. Faye wastes no time in asking me if she's considered a harlot if she sleeps with a guy on the second date. "Good grief Faye, are the sheets cold yet? I mean didn't what's his name just leave? Did he even leave the bed?" I said flopping on the sofa giggling. "See, I knew you'd start preaching," Faye said. Dang Chelle, I'm lonely. I am not ashamed to say that I love having a man lying next to me at night."

Michelle tucks her feet beneath her and gets ready for the story. "Anyway, he is so nice Chelle. He sent me flowers at work today and he must've called four times already." Faye said. Michelle can't stand the fact that Faye is so gullible. "So, do your legs have an automatic fly open policy whenever someone is nice to you? Faye, why don't you see what he's about first? Like, what's his last name? Does he have any kids? More importantly, is he married!?" I said. "Look Chelle, I don't know. I just met the man; I can't give him the third degree. I am not trying to scare him off. Girl, he wants to take me out to dinner. What should I wear? My lavender dress comes off easily." I could hear her frantically going through her closet. "You are such a skank" I say playfully. "Shut up mama Chelle, you know you a hot butt too. I mean, we can't even call the house after 9 because you and Anthony are having "alone time" Faye said. WHATeva! I'm hot for my husband." I said. Anthony comes into the room and takes a seat next to Michelle on the sofa. "Uh Hmm... Come on baby, how long you gone be?" he says, giving me a pitiful look. "Look Faye, I'll talk to you tomorrow. Use your best judgment." I said. "Does that mean I shouldn't give him none?" Faye asks. "You know it does Faye." Faye sighs and tells me that I am no fun at all. "Bye woman, love ya" I say. "Bye yourself, love you too" she says. We hang up and I turn to Anthony and whisper, "now, on to some unfinished business."

Chapter 3
Am I Wearing a Cape?

Alyssa is thirteen and is proving to be a great help with her little brothers. Lil Anthony helps too but he cherishes the few minutes in the evenings he gets to watch television. At nine years old, he often has both math and reading homework, plus whatever project they are working on to complete in the evenings and he has to read aloud for at least twenty minutes. "I swear sometimes I want to call his teacher and remind her that he's only in the 4th grade".

I walked into Alyssa's room, which is a complete mess. "Hey, baby. What's going on?" I say while lying down next to her in bed. "Nothing much, my cell phone is acting up again." Alyssa set up and pouted. She hit the phone with the palm of her hand in an effort to get it to cooperate. "Ma please, please can I get a new one? This thing is so ancient. You promised when I turned thirteen, if my grades were decent, I could get a new one. I asked Daddy and he said that if you said it was OK then I could get one. Pretty please mommy." Alyssa whined hugging me around my neck. "Ugh, begging doesn't become you missy. Give your brother a bath and I'll think about it" I say. "What other menial tasks do I have to do?" Allysa asks rubbing noses with her mom like they did when she was a tike. "Oh, I can find plenty of stuff for you to do around here. Let's start with this room." Michelle said getting up and kicking a pile of clothes. I mean, are there rodents creating families under these crusty clothes?" I said. "All right, Ma. You've made your point. I will put the little runt in the bath for you." Alyssa huffs and tries to make a pathway through the clothes. Michelle tosses what appear to be clean clothes back on the bed. "Thanks loving daughter" I said. "Yeah, yeah," moans Alyssa.

I walk down the hall into Lil Anthony's room and he is consumed with something on the television. I remind him that he has fifteen minutes before the TV goes off. "Ma", AJ calls as he looks past me to make sure I'm alone. I've saved up forty five dollars so far and dad promised if I saved up half for my game he would give me the other half." "And?" I say knowing he's up to something. "Well, can you loan me the other sixty bucks and I will pay you back as soon as the summer comes and I start helping dad in the yard?" "I am not made of money AJ. Besides your dad's money is my money. If I gave you the other $60, we would be supplying more than half." I pop him upside the head with a pillow. "Come on Ma, I really need it." AJ begs and gives up that prize winning smile. "What is it with you heathenish children? Resulting to begging to get what you want?" Michelle says. "Is it working?" AJ asks. "Duh...nah" Michelle teases. "That's cold, Ma. That's real cold." AJ says taking the pillow from me and whacking me back. "Anywho, when your brother exits the bathroom, you should be making your way into the shower buddy. And be sure to wash the funk all the way off. I just changed these sheets."

Chapter 4
Still Got It

After the children have been scrubbed clean and lights are out, I jump in the shower and take extra special care on the extra special parts. As I walk into the room I notice Anthony has lit the oil burners and turned the lights down low. I search for the bed and rub my hands over that mountainous flesh that I love so much. "Mmmmm baby, what took you so long?" he asks. "Your youngest needed three stories and two kisses and an extra tucking before he would let me out of the room" I said. Anthony gently cupped my breast while I straddled him. After fourteen years, this man still knows my every weakness.

Our love making has always been careful and slow. It's almost as if our bodies complement each other. Our unions have come to be a thing of beauty. It's no longer about just the physical but the mental as well. Anthony has taught me the art of intimacy. That's what I love about him. He seeks to please me and in turn I am reciprocal. After a very pleasurable experience, I jump up and head to the bathroom to wash and bring the cloth back to wash Anthony and he was already snoring. When I put the warm cloth on him he didn't even stir. Oh yes baby, mama's still got it.

Chapter 5
Penny for your Thoughts

Today is Anthony's day with the kids, thank God. I have to remember to put my cell on vibrate 'cause I know he's going to call and I don't want to hear Marie's mouth. When I walk into the restaurant, Marie and Faye are already seated. "Hey black women," I say. "Hey you," they say in unison. Faye's eyes are watery and Marie has a perturbed look on her face so I know it's going to be a long lunch. "Gayle is going to be a little late. She and Erik are having a "discussion," says Marie. "What now?" I ask taking my seat. "Apparently, she has a *feeling* that something is going on. She's been getting hang-ups in the middle of the night for the last few days. Erik is as fine as Denzel and LL all wrapped up in one but he isn't worth all the grief. I mean everyone but she knows that the fool is a cheating, conniving bastard. How hard can it be to toss his ass?" Marie rifles through her purse looking for her compact. She gives Faye and irritated look that lets Faye know not to open her mouth to object. "It's not that easy Marie," I say. "Gayle and Erik have a history together." Marie looks at me like I have two heads. She leans across the table, snatches the cloth napkin and tosses it onto her lap. "Well how much proof does one need, Michelle? I mean even Ms. Gullible over here would've wised up by now." Marie says looking in Faye's direction.

Faye gives me a pleading look. "All right ladies, let's order" I say, trying to lighten the mood. Marie grunts and we both start looking at the menu. Faye excuses herself and goes to the ladies room. Marie takes her cue and whispers to Michelle. "Can you talk some since into that heffa please? She just told me that she is thinking about letting what's-his-face have a key to her house. I offered to start a background check on the mystery man and she told me I was being ridiculous. She just met this clown less than a month ago. She can't

11

be head over hills already!" I put down my menu and gave Marie my attention. "Have you met him Chelle?" Marie wanted to know. "No, I haven't" I say. "But according to Faye, he's wonderful. He has a home that she hasn't seen yet. He's a partner in a business, doing what she does not know. And he isn't married because he doesn't have a ring and she can call him any time she wants." I say. We stop talking as Faye rejoins us at the table and I spot Gayle entering the restaurant. After smooches and hello's all around, we place our orders and Gayle starts in on her latest suspicions with Erik.

"Let's get down to business ladies," Gayle starts after she makes sure we're all ears. "I knew it, I knew it!" She says fuming. "Erik is whoring around on me." We all look at each other like, what else is new. Gayle gives us the evil eye and continued. "So I left out this morning at around six since I had an early appointment with Sandy to get my naps fried" she said making sure we took notice of her new cut. "I called Erik three times at the house and then tried his cell and I couldn't get him on that either. I wasted no time leaving the salon and heading for the house to find out why the hell he wasn't answering my calls. As I was entering the gates and passing the guards station, I see this gorgeous BMW Z4 about to exit on the opposite side." Marie interrupted, "That is a gorgeous car, Gayle. Good grief, do you know how much that thing costs!?" Marie ogled. We all looked at Marie like we wanted to choke her. Here we are trying to listen to Gayle and her dilemma and all she could do was squawk about money. Marie is the most materialistic one out of all of us. "What! I'm sorry," Marie said totally oblivious to why we were perturbed. Gayle rolled her eyes at Marie and continued. "Well this familiar looking woman is in the Beemer eyeing me with this coy look like she knew me or knew something that I didn't.

So after doing the usual back and forth with Andy the guard, I casually ask who the woman was here seeing." Gayle readjusted how she was sitting in her chair and we all leaned in a little closer. "Get this, Andy who knows everything about everybody that lives there, says that the woman said she was dropping off some paperwork for Erik. I thank Andy and he gives me a knowing look like, *go take care of your business girl.* I floor it around the corner and up my driveway. I didn't open the garage because I didn't want Erik to know I was back. I hopped out like a madwoman and went in through the kitchen door and up the backstairs to our bedroom. Erik was in the shower and it smelled awfully strange in there." We are all hanging on to Gayle's every word as the waiter gives us our food and we wave him away. Gayle goes on, "I walk into the bathroom and snatched open the shower door. I was like "what the hell is going on up in here!" He almost broke his neck 'cause I scared the living you know what out of him." We all laughed and got curious stares from the people in the restaurant. Gayle continued, "He was all like, "baby what are you doing back so soon? I thought you were at the hairdresser." I promptly slapped the mess out of him and asked him why it smelled like a dirty woman in my bedroom. Of course he was dumbfounded. I tell him to get out of the shower right now because it was about to be some furniture moving up in there! He finally comes out of the bathroom and walked in the bedroom with his towel on still wet. I asked him why my bed was a mess when I know I made it before I left. "What did he say girl," asks Faye. We all nod egging her on.

"*Apparently*, he got tired after "working out" and wanted to grab a quick nap. Since I know he is as vain as any woman, I asked him if he got in my bed funky after working out. He was like "uhhhh, no." So I was like "well if you worked out and then took a nap, why the hell were you just showering?" Of course he had nothing to say. I asked him who was the hooch that just left in the BMW? He looked at me like is this wench psychic or something? Stuttering he said, "That's Pam, she works with me Gayle. What's up with the third degree and why the hell did you slap me?" He said rubbing his face. "Why was she here Erik," I say. "Uh, she wanted to speak to me about some proposals." He says. I came back with, "you have a trio, a desk top, and a personal cell phone. You mean to tell me she couldn't send you an email? Did she have to come over on a Saturday to your residence to speak to you about a proposal? This couldn't wait until Monday morning when you took your black ass in to work?" I asked. "I told him to be up and outta my house by the time I finished my meal with you all. And I mean it this time yall. I am so sick and tired of his excuses."

Marie tries to conceal what she really wanted to say which is, *it's about friggin time*. But instead she says, "Baby girl, we are here for you whatever you decide to do." I chime in with, "we love you Gayle. We can't stand to see what this is doing to you. You are all stressed out all of the time. Have you guys ever thought about counseling?" Gayle grunted. "He won't go. He says that he doesn't want some stranger judging him. He thinks I'm over dramatizing about everything." Her eyes start to tear and she yanks a tissue from her purse. "He keeps telling me that I am imagining things." Faye asked what we were all wondering, "What will you do if he leaves, Gayle? I mean, your house is huge. Can you afford to stay if Erik leaves." Gayle looks up and puts her hands on her hips. "Hell yeah I could afford it. I mean, it would be a struggle but I am not losing my home." Gayle states matter-of-factly. We sat in silence for a moment until finally Marie lifts her water glass and proposed a toast. "To life and the changes that are sure to come!" We all saluted and commenced to eating. Everyone gave their updates about what was going on with them. By the time we finished our meal, the mood had lightened.

On the way out of the restaurant and to our cars Marie gives me a look that tells me she will be calling me to discuss lunch. We all give smooches and hugs and go our separate ways. I dig my cell out of my purse and call Anthony at the house to tell him I'm on my way home. He tells me that I sound tired and I agree. He promised we could take a nap when I get there because my mom stopped by and took the kids to a movie. I exceed the speed limit all the way there breathing a sigh of relief as I finally hit the button for the garage opener.

Chapter 6
Is This a Luv Thang?

"So baby, do you think I could come over to your house with you?
You told me last week that we would spend this weekend at your
house" Faye asked Calvin. For the past two months, Calvin came to
her house after work. They hadn't gone out yet but Faye just figured
he'd been tired or just wanted to get to know her. Calvin caught an
immediate attitude. "Damn Faye! Why you always on a brotha's
back? I mean I told you that I'm getting some work done on the
house. Why do you think we always kick it here at your place?"
Calvin replies. Faye walked around the couch to gently massage his
shoulders as he watched television in his boxers. "I just want to see
your world baby. I mean all we ever do is order in, watch movies
and screw" Faye said. Calvin looked over at her. He knew this
would happen. Eventually all women got nosey and controlling and
had to be put in their place. "Do you have a problem with that Faye?
I mean I'm here with you aren't I? I'm not out clubbing or spending
my time with other women" he said. He snatched away from her
and got up to go the fridge to get another beer. "You need to go to
the store. This is the last beer and are you planning on cooking me
something to eat or do we have to order take out again?" Calvin
wanted to know. "No, I'm thawing pork chops in the fridge." Faye
said. "Well I don't want pork chops; I would like to have spaghetti.
You still have time or is that too much to ask?" he said and slammed
the door to the fridge and walked back into the living room. Faye
didn't want him to be mad at her. She went to the pantry and got
him some chips to go with his beer. Then she took out ground
turkey and threw it in the microwave so that it would thaw faster.
She'd promised Michelle and Anthony that she would watch the kids
while they went out to dinner, but Calvin is still here and she didn't
want to make him uncomfortable.

Faye took the cordless into the bathroom to call Michelle and break the news that they'd have to find another sitter for tonight. She hated confrontation. Her best friend rarely had time to go out and she hated to disappoint her. "Hey Chelle, what's up?" Faye could tell by Chelle's hesitation that she sensed something was wrong. "Look Chelle, I may have to back out of watching the babies tonight." Faye took the phone from her ear so that Chelle wouldn't burst her eardrum. "Yes, I know that I promised, sis. Yes, I know you confirmed the date twice. It's just that Calvin is here and he's a little stressed from work and I know he'd like to relax. Yes Chelle, Calvin does have his own place. Look, maybe next.....hello. Chelle?" Faye slid down onto the floor and couldn't hold in the sobs as tears streamed down her face. Michelle was the last one Faye wanted to let down. Couldn't Chelle see that she wanted this relationship to work? Just as Faye was about to press redial, Calvin tried to turn the door knob. "Faye, this spaghetti isn't going to fix itself. I'm starving like Marvin out here baby. Come on and feed your man and later on I'll feed you some of this beef right here." He said while grabbing his manhood. Faye gathered herself and stuck the cordless in the medicine cabinet so he wouldn't know she was on the phone. She swatted at her eyes, spruced up her hair and opened the door to Calvin holding himself. God bless him. He was working with a lot of beef.

Chapter 7
The Scheme of Things

Marie took a moment before going into the meeting with her staff.
She had to admit, she'd done good. The new sitting area of the book
store was fabulous. Designed with warm earth tone colors and plush
couches and chairs gave customers a warm, comfy feeling. She
wanted to create a relaxing atmosphere so that customers wouldn't
want to leave. If her parents were alive today, they'd be so pleased
with what she'd accomplished. As she walked into the store's small
meeting room, she was ready for business as usual. Marie had a
staff of four. Liz, the manager, Monique the customer service rep,
Cheri the café attendant and Stephanie, the floor assistant were all
young women either in college or fresh out.

Marie stood in front of her chair at the mahogany conference table
and placed her notepad and the copy of the book on the table. She
folded her hands on the back of the leather chair and got started with
the business at hand. "All right ladies, today's agenda is to discuss
the illustrious author, Mr. Parnell Hawkins, who will be gracing our
lovely establishment tomorrow. The book signing is from 12 noon
until 2 pm right?" She said glancing at the notes that she knew by
heart. "Monique, you will be in charge of getting Mr. Hawkins
anything that he needs. Stephanie, your task will be organizing the
mob of women that will be fighting for his attention. Cheri, you will
continue to work the café and keep a hot cup of java in everyone's
hand. Lastly, Liz you did a great job from the promotional side. Do
you have the schedule for the local radio stations ready for me?" Liz
slid the schedule over to Marie. "Also, the car and driver need to be
at the hotel at least 15 minutes before hand. You can work with Mr.
Hawkins assistant to make sure you guys are on the same page. The
transition from one station to the other needs to be a smooth one, I
don't want him to feel rushed or put out by any means." Marie

looked over the schedule noting a few changes that needed to be made. She'd volunteered to have her staff take care of Mr. Hawkins transportation during his stay.

"Did you ladies read the book yet?" Marie asked finally taking her seat. *Borderline Blues* had been on the number one sellers list for 3 months. "I loved it," Stephanie said. "It didn't hurt that Parnell is gorgeous!" Everyone agreed that the man had it going on. "Well, let's get it all out now. When he gets here I don't want everyone tripping over themselves." Marie warned. She put the tip of her pen in her mouth and swiveled in her chair a bit. "You know, I hear he's single Marie. And you are looking especially fabulous here lately. What's up with that?" said Cheri. Marie rolled her eyes at the comment. "Please girl. I am simply putting my best foot forward. I want Mr. Hawkins to know that even though we are a small establishment, we are equally competent to hang with the big dogs. Besides, who told you that he was single?" Marie asked slyly. "We all read the article that was in People magazine last week." Cheri says sliding the magazine to Marie. "Well, good for him. All right you battleaxes, let's get to work." Marie grabbed the article along with the rest of her things and headed to her office.

"Please be on time today OK ladies. I really need you guys support on this one. I need my girls here in case stuff doesn't go right." Marie said as she massaged her temples with her feet on her mahogany desk. They were all on a conference call listening to Marie stress about the book signing. Parnell Hawkins was due to arrive shortly and she was stressing as usual. "We wouldn't miss it for the world," Michelle said. You won't have time to say two words to us anyway. You'll be busy *entertaining* Mr. Hawkins." Michelle said teasingly. "Don't start it OK. I do not need any more pressure. Who even said that I liked the man? So what he wrote a book. So what he looks good enough to eat." Marie said checking her hose for runs. Today was the big day and she was so nervous she wasn't able to eat anything this morning. "Should I just throw myself at the man? Everyone is making it seem like I'm desperate and destitute. Give me a little credit" Marie stated. "Well he has sent you flowers every day this week Marie. It's obvious he's interested" said Michelle. "He just wants to make a good impression, that's all. This is the first time we'll be meeting. We've only had telephone conversations about the signing and all of the other specifics. This is very important to me and I want everything to go well" Marie said exasperated . "We'll be there at 11:30 am sharp!" said Faye. "Alyssa said she hopes you're wearing that brown suite that you guys picked up at the mall the other day. She said it was fierce! Is it true that it makes you look like the woman on the cover of the book?" Michelle asked. Marie got up and looked at herself in the large mirror in her office and agreed with Alyssa, she was doin' the doggon thing in this suit. If all goes well today, she would treat Alyssa to that new cell phone she'd been crying about. After all, the girl had taste when it came to clothes. "OK, so I'll see you guys here at 11:30 and no later right?" Marie said leaning back on her desk. "We'll be there," they said in unison.

After hanging up Marie tidied up her office and checked her makeup once more. Why was everyone making such a fuss over this man? He couldn't possibly be interested in a woman he's never met. He probably does this at each book signing. "This is purely professional" Marie said as she smoothed her suit out once more and headed for the door. "Strictly business, nothing more." Then why was she so friggin' nervous…

Chapter 8
Madness and Mayhem

"Ooh Marie, I have never seen so many women in one place since Luther was in town, bless his heart" said Gayle. "The café is marvelous girl. We are so proud of you" said Michelle. Marie beamed with pride. "Do you really think everything is going all right? The line has been out the door since I opened at nine this morning" Marie said. "You tell us, I've had to help Cheri at the café since opening, Monique has had to restock the books five times already and poor Stephanie was almost accosted when she had to tell all of the women that they needed to wait in line" said Michelle giggling.

"Faye has been helping at the register and staying as close to Parnell as possible. She probably wants advice on how to write a self-help book now" Marie said. "Leave her alone. Marie, this has been a great turn out. I saw Jessie Hayes from the Post taking notes. I'm sure the write up will be superb." Michelle said. "Well, it's time for Parnell's break so I'll see you guys in a few" Marie says. Gayle and Michelle playfully fixed Marie's skirt and spruced up her hair. "Would you lunatics stop?! You all are driving me crazy." Marie said trying to get away from them. "How's my makeup?" Marie says as she smiles and puckers her lips and wipes under her eyes for traces of eyeliner. "You look great Ms. Marie. You'd better go on, Stephanie looks like she could use a break too" Michelle said. "I'll run interference."

Chapter 9
Back at One

"So Parnell, I'm sure you'd agree that the signing was a great success." Marie stated as she situated herself at the dining table of the Sequoia restaurant with a beautiful view of the water. After the signing, Marie offered to take him to a congratulatory dinner. "Please give credit where credit is due. Ms. Johnson, you are the epitome of professionalism. Don't think I didn't see you working your magic. You had this thing planned with no room for errors. And for that, I thank you." He said with a nod in her direction. "It was my pleasure just watching you" Parnell said with just a hint of flirtation. For a moment Marie was lost in his eyes. The way he spoke and his body movements demanded attention. She sat up a little straighter. *Get it together Marie*, she said to herself. *What is wrong with me? I am always in control. Where the hell is the waiter when you needed him anyway?* "Marie? Marie, is everything alright?" Parnell asked touching her hand. "Uh...what? Oh yes, everything is fine Parnell. I'm so happy you were satisfied..., I mean happy with the way things turned out. I have a wonderful staff and my best friends helped me out a lot today" Marie stated nervously.

Parnell picked up the menu. "Well, shall we order?" Parnell asked looking over the menu. "What do you feel like this evening?" Parnell asked. He enjoyed watching Marie squirm a little. Marie looked at the menu but was thinking that she could tell him what she felt like all right. *Good grief, is it hot in here or is it me.* "Uh, I'll have the roasted lamb and a garden salad," Marie said. "Well then," Parnell said as he signaled the waiter. "I'd be happy to order for us. I suggest red wine with that. Is that all right with you sweet lady?" "Why yes Parnell, that'd be fine." *Lord please help me to keep my composure. You'd think I hadn't been on a date in years. Not that this is a date though. This is merely a meal between colleagues. What do we talk about? Good heavens, are we sitting under a heat lamp*, Marie thought as she resituated herself in her seat. "So Parnell, how long are you in town?" she asked. He relaxed in his chair and took a piece of bread out of the bread basket to butter. "I actually have a home here in Washington. I used to live here as a child so the house has been in my family for more than 50 years. I recently restored it and I try to come home at least three times a year. So far, nothing has made me want to stay longer. Until now, that is" he said. Marie couldn't help but blush. "Are you flirting with me young man?" Marie blushed. "I'm trying hard as hell Marie. How's my game? I'm a little rusty with this whole mackin' thing." he smiled. Thank God our food arrived. Marie excused herself to go to the ladies room to cool off and gain some control. *Whew! I need to get out more often.*

They had a wonderful time. Marie forgot how fun going out could be. "Thanks so much for dinner Parnell. You really should've allowed me to pay seeing as though I invited you. You were a perfect gentleman" Marie said as they neared her front door. "No need to thank me, Marie. I was the envy of every man at the restaurant tonight. Did I tell you how stunning you look?" Parnell asked admiring her once more. He'd never met a woman so poised. "As a matter of fact you did, but feel free to tell me again." Marie said blushing a little. "You are quite a woman Marie Johnson. I'd love to see you again, outside of work that is." Parnell said. "I look forward to it." Marie said. Parnell grabbed both of her hands and gently kissed them both. Marie thought for sure she stumbled a bit. "I'll give you a call most definitely." Parnell said. As he returned to his car Marie went into the house and almost flipped over the sofa trying to get to the phone. She had five messages from the three stooges. Marie decided that it was too late to call and give them the details. She also didn't want to seem too excited about Parnell. After all, she didn't want to make a big deal about nothing. If he called that would be fine. If he didn't that would be fine also. She wasn't going to lose any sleep over it. Marie went upstairs to shower and get ready for bed. Before she went into the bathroom she checked the bedroom phone to make sure the ringer was on.

Chapter 10
Something in the Water

"AJ, please dump and wash the wastebaskets and the large cans in the garage. Michael can help you dump them." Michelle gathered all of her cleaning supplies from the closet. Michael waited for her to give him something to do. Michelle noticed him and said, "Michael, can you help your brother dump the trash cans for Mommy?" AJ frowned and said, "He'll just be in the way Mom. I got it." Michael pouted and crossed his arms across his chest. "I can do it AJ! Am I in the way Mommy?" Michael wanted to know. Michelle bent down so that they'd be eye to eye. "Of course not sweet pea," she said while throwing daggers at AJ. AJ moaned and told Michael to come on. "You'd better not drop anything either" he said. Michelle continued dishing out orders. "Alyssa, get the vacuum out for me and then start separating the clothes." She said entering her room. "OK Mom but can I watch this video first? I want to learn how to do this dance to put in my number for the recital." Alyssa stood in front of the TV mimicking the girl in the video. Michelle looked over at the TV and frowned. She bumped Alyssa with her hip and said, "There won't be a recital for you if your legs are broken. Now move young lady" she said. Alyssa stumbled a bit in mock pain. "Whoa, what's with the violence Mom?" she said. Hey, did I tell you that auntie Marie is going to get me the cell phone I wanted?" Alyssa said as she started gathering clothes from everyone's laundry baskets. Michelle said, "Yes, she mentioned getting it since you were such a big help with the book signing. You did a great job helping her to clean the store and shop for something to wear, so that will be her thank you for a job well done. Now, those clothes aren't going to separate themselves.

"What time is recital practice today?" Michelle asked over her shoulder as she walked down the hall. "Two o'clock. We have a new assistant instructor. His name is Terrell. He is supposed to be some renowned dancer." Alyssa said making a grand gesture. "Well, we have a lot to do this morning so let's get this house in order." Michelle said. Alyssa struggled with the clothes hamper as she followed her mom. "Mom, I think you may be a little obsessive compulsive. This house is already squeaking it's so clean. Daddy says that he's afraid to sit on his own bed for fear you'll clobber him for sitting on the comforter." Alyssa said. Michelle stopped in her tracks and Alyssa nearly ran into the back of her with the clothes hamper. "Oh, so you and Dad are conspiring against me, ha? He knows that I don't want him sitting on the bed in his work clothes. At bed time don't you want to sleep on nice good smelling sheets?" Michelle continued on into the bathroom. "And what is so wrong with keeping a clean house anyway? You all will thank me for this one day missy! Humph…I'm going to start on my bathrooms" Michelle said as she walked into the bathroom. She shook her head in disgust. "I swear it's like those boys, including your dad, wear blindfolds when they use the bathroom. They can't seem to point those things in the right direction." Alyssa frowned and pinched her nose and took the clothes down to the laundry room.

Anthony popped his head into the bathroom. "Do I have a honey-do list baby or am I free and clear?" Michelle was spraying the bath tub and Anthony took the opportunity to swat her on the bottom. Michelle turned on him with the bathroom cleaner in hand and pointed in his direction. "Anthony, did you tell the kids that I'm obsessive compulsive? Don't you like having a clean home?" she said obviously annoyed. Anthony didn't realize what he walked in on. He put up his hands in defeat. "Sweetheart, I was kidding with the kids this morning. I know you run a tight ship and I love that about you. Come on now." He pulled her to him and planted hugs and kisses. "We couldn't survive without you. I know I couldn't." He let go of her and turned to leave. He waited until he was in the clear before he said, "I am afraid to sit on the bed when it's all made up though. That was not a lie." He said laughing. "WHATever man. Hey listen, I need you to fix the faucet in the downstairs bathroom and the bulb in the ceiling fan is out in the kitchen." By this time Anthony was down the stairs and had almost made it out of the door. He went back and stood at the bottom of the stairs. "Then can AJ and I go take care of some things in the garage and out back your highness?" "I guess so, you traitor" Michelle said.

Chapter 11
Kiss and Tell

Michelle walked into the jazz club and took a seat at the bar. Several guys took note of her in a classic black dress that hit all of her curves nicely. It had a plunging neckline that gave way to her voluptuous bosom. "Can I have something fruity and not too strong please?" Michelle asked as the bartender neared. "Sure pretty lady. Are you dining alone tonight?" asked the bartender. Michelle looked around. "I guess it looks that way doesn't it" she said mischievously. She slowly sipped her drink and enjoyed the music. Several gentlemen asked her to dance to which she kindly declined. This was the first night in a long time that she had to herself. She noticed a good looking guy on the other side of the room. They kept making eye contact. He was dressed in a black turtle neck and black slacks with a smoke gray sport coat. He sat nursing his drink and looking at her. She felt like a bad girl because she flirted with her eyes and body language. Michelle must've been at the bar for about an hour when finally the gentleman asked her to dance. Since her evening was nearing a close she figured it couldn't hurt anything to have at least one dance.

The other men looked on with envy as this tall, dark and handsome creature escorted her to the dance floor and took her languidly in his arms. They expertly moved on the dance floor as if they were meant to be together. His hands slowly moved closer to her bottom and she playfully slid them back up to the small of her back. He pulled her a little closer and she rested her head on his shoulder. Umph, this felt all too good. He asked her why such a beautiful woman was here alone tonight. She told him that she felt a little unappreciated and decided to treat herself to a night out alone. "How could a man not appreciate a woman of such style and beauty?" he wanted to know. "I thought maybe I was losing my sex appeal. Perhaps he isn't as attracted to me as he once was" Michelle replied. "He's a fool if he lets you slip through his fingers. Would you mind if I showed you a night you won't soon forget?" Michelle blushed. "What did you have in mind?" As the band finished the number, he led her off of the dance floor. "Just relax and let me help you feel appreciated. There's a nice hotel near here. You could leave your car here and I could bring you back later. I promise to be the perfect gentleman." he said looking into her eyes. "You don't even know my name." Michelle replied feeling a little nervous. "That isn't important" he replied. He took her by the hand and led her to the exit. "Hey man, that brother must have a helluva pick up line. I've been trying to talk to her all night" two men conversed as the couple passed them.

As they made their way to his car, Anthony pulled Michelle close and slowly kissed her. "You look hot as hell in that dress baby." He said. "What took you so long to ask me to dance?" Michelle asked playfully hitting him. "Seeing those other men drool over you was too amusing to pass up. I wanted to enjoy it a little longer" Anthony teased. "Humph, I should've danced with one of those guys just to teach you a lesson." Michelle said. "I knew who you were leaving with baby." He said as he held her close. "When did you get this dress?!" He couldn't get enough of looking at her. It made him want her even more. "When you walked in the guy next to me almost spilled his drink on himself trying to get a closer look." Anthony spun her around. "Anthony, I've had this dress since forever. Come on, let's go. It's getting cold out here" Michelle said hugging herself. He helped her into the car and they drove to a little bed and breakfast not far from there.

He'd gone earlier and placed rose petals all over the room. He had Gayle help him buy a negligee that he couldn't wait to rip off of her. Chocolate covered strawberries and champagne were chilling by the bed. Scented candles surrounded the Jacuzzi. Massage oils and candlelight was only some of what she'd be getting tonight. He had plans to bathe her, massage all of the tension out of her body and make sweet love to her all night long.

From the moment they met, Anthony knew he had to have her. There was something about her that made people flock to her. She

27

had this strong willed nature that was sexy as hell. He thought that she was too good for him but he would do whatever he had to do to have her. She was six years his junior and had plans and dreams. He was a hardworking man that didn't mind getting his hands dirty. He didn't have a pocket full of money and he didn't dress to impress. Instead he saved so that one day he could open his own business and give her everything that she deserved. He'd walk her home from the bus stop. Pick her up nights when she had late classes. He'd shoot the breeze with her parents and help fix things around their house. All so that he could have a few moments with her. Now that he had her, there was nothing he wouldn't do for her. He wanted her to know that. After fifteen years, she still was everything he ever wanted.

Chapter 12
The One

"Who the hell told you to call my place of business Faye?" Calvin
asked as he backed Faye up against the wall in her foyer. "You got
those fools clowning me like I'm a chump or something." Faye had
called earlier and the receptionist thought that it was funny when
she'd asked if she was Calvin's assistant. Faye made it a point to tell
her that she was his girlfriend and she wanted to surprise him for
lunch. She told Faye that Calvin didn't need an assistant to clean the
offices. He could do that all by himself. Faye thought she was
kidding and didn't give it another thought until now. Faye couldn't
look him in the eye. He frightened her and she tried to think of the
right thing to say. Why did he have to lie to her? He told her that he
was a head consultant at a construction firm. She saw a pen in one
of his pants pockets that said A&M Construction and she memorized
the telephone number. "I only called to see how your day was
going. I was going to bring you lunch. Why is it such a big deal
anyway?" Faye asked. It came out of nowhere. Faye didn't realize
he'd hit her until she looked up in a daze from the floor and he was
standing over her. The right side of her face felt like someone had
slapped her with a frying pan. She struggled to sit up as she held her
face. "I know you did not just put your damn hands on me Calvin!"
Faye scrambled to her feet still feeling a little dizzy. "Have you lost
your mind or something?" Calvin grabbed the sides of his head.
"I'm sorry Faye. I didn't mean to hit you baby...let me see your
face" Calvin said trying to touch her face. Faye slapped his hand
away. "I think you should leave Calvin" she said. "Get the hell out
of my house now!" she yelled as tears streamed down her swollen
face.

Faye walked up the stairs into her bedroom and slammed the door.
"Faye" he called after her. "Faye, wait a minute." Calvin ran up the

29

stairs behind her and banged on her bedroom door. "Can we just talk about this please?" he asked. Faye paced the floor holding herself. "How could you hit me Calvin? I thought you were different!" Faye cried. He tried to coax her out of the room. "Baby open the door. Let's talk about this. I really didn't mean to hurt you. You know I have a temper, Faye. Open the door and let me look at your face." He knocked a little softer this time. Faye sat on her bed and looked at her face in the mirror. How in the hell could she go to work looking like this tomorrow. She knew she should make his ass leave but he sounded so pitiful. Maybe she should just listen to what he had to say. He did tell her not to ever call his job because personal calls were frowned upon. He told her to always call his cell. Why did she always have to push? She slowly walked over to the bedroom door. She grabbed the door knob and then let go. "Please Faye, let me make it up to you baby. I promise I will keep my temper in check. Come on, baby. Open up." Calvin begged. She couldn't hold out any longer. She slowly turned the door knob. Calvin was sitting on the floor with his head on her door. When she opened the door he grabbed her around the waist and cried like a baby. "I'm so sorry baby. Please don't shut me out. You all I got, Faye. I don't have anyone else." Calvin cried. Faye slid to the floor beside him and laid his head in her lap. "I'm sorry I called your job Calvin. I wasn't trying to put you on the spot. I just wanted you to know that I was thinking about you baby, that's all." They sat like that for what seemed like hours.

Finally, Calvin stood up and picked her up in his arms and carried her to the bed. He peeled her clothes from her, laid her on the bed and stood back looking at her without saying a word. Faye was starting to feel a little uncomfortable and was about to cover herself. "Don't move baby. I just want to look at you" he said. "You are so beautiful, Faye. I don't deserve you baby." Calvin started to take his clothes off. Standing naked at the foot of the bed, he took himself in his hands and gently stroked himself while looking at her. He slowly climbed onto the bed and entered her. With each stroke he told her how sorry he was. Deep inside, Faye could tell he really meant it. She was so pushy at times. She'd have to learn to stop moving so fast. It was obvious he cared for her. He spent all of his free time with her after all. Yep, she would take her time with this one. Show him that she was willing to wait for him. I mean, good men are hard to find, right? Lord knows he felt good. Toxic even. Afterwards they lay side by side. "I love you Calvin," Faye said. When she didn't get a response, she looked over at him and he had fallen off to sleep. Or at least she thought he was sleeping.

Chapter 13
The Sense of a Penny

"Can you try her once more please Ann?" Michelle asked her assistant. "Sure Michelle," Ann replied. Why hadn't Faye returned any of her phone calls? Gayle hadn't talked to her in a couple of days either and Marie couldn't remember the last time she'd talked to her. What is going on with that girl? She'd called in sick both Monday and Tuesday. Now here it is Wednesday and her office claimed she was in meetings all day. Michelle hoped she hadn't been too hard on Faye when she backed out of taking care of the kids. This new guy she'd been seeing must really be something. Hopefully this one will see her worth and treat her the way she should be treated. Guys these days were so scandalous. "Her voicemail says that she'll be in meetings until three Michelle." Ann said over the intercom. "Would you like for me to leave her another message?" she asked. Michelle pushed down the button. "No Ann. Thanks so much. I'll try to reach her later at home." Michelle made a mental note to stop by Faye's if she didn't talk to her before close of business.

"How in the hell am I going to go into work looking like this?" Faye stood in front of the vanity mirror in her bathroom. Calvin was still sleeping since he didn't have to be at work until noon today. What the hell kinda job allows you to come in at different times during the week? Did he really clean the offices like the receptionist claimed? She remembered him saying he was a partner or a consultant or something. She'd make it a point to bring up work again to see if she could get a better idea as to what he did with himself when he wasn't with her. As she walked back into the bedroom she watched him sleeping. He lay peacefully on his side looking so comfortable, she hated to wake him. Maybe she should take another day off. Her face looked like she had an abscessed tooth.

32

She had to smile when she thought of how Calvin made up for hitting her over and over again. He'd said this weekend they would stay at his house finally. He'd even promised to introduce her to his mom in the near future. They'd been seeing each other for almost three months now and she had no clue as to what his life was like. All she knew was that he wasn't close to his family and didn't associate with too many people. He was engaged once but she cheated on him. That's why he was so guarded with relationships. "Baby, I'm gone." She said as she bent over him and kissed him with his morning breath. He groaned and turned over and put his back to her. Faye glanced in the mirror on her way to her bedroom door. "I set the alarm for eight and your breakfast is in the microwave. Have a great day." She turned to leave the bedroom and stopped again. "Will I see you later this evening?" She asked hopeful. "We'll see" he said. He said that he had some errands that he needed to run. She thought to ask if she could go with him and then thought better of it. "OK, well I'll talk to you later." Once in the car she checked in her wallet to see if she had enough for parking and lunch. She was sure she had about forty dollars but her wallet was empty. She checked her entire purse but thought maybe she forgot it when she changed purses or something. Now she would have to stop at the bank on the way in to work.

Faye had meetings most of the day. She knew the girls had been trying to reach her since Sunday when she missed church. She didn't have the heart to talk to them. She knew Michelle would see right through her. Hopefully, her face would be back to normal by this Sunday's service. Maybe she'd see if Calvin would join her at church. Lord knows we all need a little Jesus every now and then. As she drove to work she perfected her ailment. She knew all of their nosy asses would be stalking about wondering why she was off when she usually never took off of work. She'd just run in and grab her briefs, have her assistant complete a couple of assignments, check her voicemails and emails and then jet. Calvin should be getting up right about now. Maybe she should call him and see how he was enjoying his breakfast that she prepared and put in the microwave. And, she just wanted to tell him that she loved him. Just as she was dialing, her boss walked in. As she cradled the

33

phone she made a mental note to check Calvin's wallet for a home address and to see what else she could find. What could it hurt?

Chapter 14
Sanctified

Only your very best for God, is what my mama always says.
Dressed in their Sunday's best, Anthony, Michelle and their brood
where making our way to their usual section of seats. Michelle was
keeping an eye out for Marie, Gayle and Faye. She had a couple of
choice words for Faye when she saw her today. She had the nerve
not calling all week like she had an attitude or something. The
opening hymn was uplifting as usual. Everyone was asked to stand
and sing, *Standing in the Need of Prayer*. Michelle casually put her
coat and purse a little ways down the pew to save room for her girls.
She and Anthony sat with Michael in between them. AJ and Alyssa
went down to children's church since it was the first Sunday.

A few minutes went by before she saw Gayle and Marie making
their way towards them. Michelle moved her things to make room
and quickly glanced back to see if she saw Faye behind them. "Is
Faye with you guys?" she whispered to Gayle as she sat next to her.
Gayle shook her head no and said, "I called her this morning and got
her answering machine. I wanted to know if she wanted me to swing
by and pick her up since I volunteered to drive today." Gayle
whispered sliding out of her coat. Marie leaned across Gayle so that
she could talk to Chelle. "Just leave it alone and stop worrying
yourself crazy. She's in love now Chelle. Her nose is wide open.
You know how she gets when she has a man." Marie said sitting
back up and glancing at the program. Michelle looked around again.
"I'm just a little worried. The last time I spoke to her she sounded
strange, like something wasn't right. You know how I get these
feelings" Michelle said. Anthony gently nudged her shoulder
shushing her as the pastor took the podium.

At the end of the sermon, the pastor asked for individuals in need of prayer to join him at the alter. Michelle busied herself reading the scripture lesson that pastor suggested that they look over when she heard crying from the front of the church. There were several people standing at the alter and Michelle had to look round them. There was a woman was on her knees as the pastor began praying. Whoever it was must've had a tremendous weight on her shoulders. The woman's shoulders shook with grief as the elders of the church surrounded her and the others to offer comfort. Michelle tried to see who it was when Marie reached across Gayle, yanked her hand whispering that it was Faye at the altar. Michelle looked and was shocked to see Faye with tears running down her face while she tried unsuccessfully to pat at her eyes with crumpled tissue. Michelle got up to go to her when Anthony stopped her. "Maybe she needs this time, baby. Let her make her peace and you all can talk to her after service" Anthony said. Michelle hesitated a minute and then decided he was right. After the prayer the ones gathered at the front took their seats. Faye sat at the end of their pew and Marie put her arm around her shoulders.

After service, we all made our way to the vestibule. "The choir tore it up today" Gayle belted as they waited outside for the children to come out of children's church. "It was nothing like the gospel choir though. Chelle when you sing solo there isn't a dry eye in the house" Marie said. "That's right. My baby sings like an angel" Anthony said hugging Michelle. She blushed and looked at Faye standing quietly to the side looking lost. Gayle and Michelle made their way over to her. "Hey you. I missed you last week. I must've left 100 messages at work and at home. What's up, are you all right?" Michelle wanted to know. Faye smiled and sighed. "I'm fine Chelle. I'm just trying to make things work with Calvin." she said. "You look like you have a lot on your mind. I'd like to help if I can." Michelle said. Faye glanced at Anthony and said "I'm just tired Chelle. I'm ready to settle down and it just never seems to work out for me. It's so hard to find a good man these days. What's wrong with me Chelle? Why doesn't he love me the way that I love him?" Faye said. By this time Marie had made her way over to them. Marie hugged Faye. "I don't care what you do for a man; he has to love you just because. I truly believe that." The amen corner agreed. "Be patient," Marie said. "He's out there. Sometimes not as perfect as we'd like but trust he's out there." Gayle and Michelle looked at Marie and wondered what was up with her and Parnell these days. She was the new found expert on men all of a sudden. Parnell had clearly changed her view on things.

The kids bounded out of the church and we began to head our separate ways. We agreed on a restaurant for our weekly get together, kissed and hugged and found our cars. Alyssa nudged me as we loaded into the car, "Mom, what's up with Auntie Faye? She barely had two words for us today. She didn't even say anything about my new outfit." She said checking herself out in the reflection of the car. "Probably man trouble again" mumbled AJ. Michelle frowned at AJ and said "She just wasn't feeling too well today that's all." She glanced back at the kids to see if they were buying the story. "Does her belly hurt Mommy?" Michael wanted to know. "I'm not sure baby, but I'm sure she'll be fine. Now, what do you all want for dinner tonight?" Anthony was first "A Gospel Bird would be great." he said rubbing his belly as he started the car. "No daddy we want a roast." This was from AJ and Alyssa. "I want ice cream" said Michael licking his lips. We all looked at him and giggled. I said a silent thank you to God for giving me such a great family. Lord only knows we have our issues but nothing we haven't been able to conquer so far.

Chapter 15
Silky Smooth

"Parnell, last night was lovely. Thank you so much for everything, you were great." Marie said as she handed him his coat and walked him to the front door. "Marie honey, you make it sound like I just helped you hang some new pictures around the house. Last night was a beautiful thing. Don't put it off like it was anything but that. We made beautiful love, woman." Parnell said wrapping his arms around her. Marie looked out the front door hoping the neighbors weren't watching. "You have to loosen up some Marie. Let them watch…maybe we could teach them something." He kissed her long and hard right there in broad daylight where all the nosy neighbors could see. Marie held back at first but eventually couldn't deny how good he felt. As Parnell walked to his car, she readjusted her bath robe and patted down her hair. What was this man doing to her? He seemed so sure of himself. His confidence and ability to control any environment he was in excited the hell out of her. She waved goodbye to him as he got into his car. *Grab a hold of yourself Marie, you all are simply friends and nothing else,* she smiled at him as he backed out of her drive way. She turned to go back inside and closed the door. *Besides, he lives in a different city for goodness sakes. New York certainly isn't around the corner.* She'd have to tell him that they should slow up a little. There was a lot at stake here.

It was finally Friday and Marie wanted to get an early start. As she got dressed, she remembered the last time she was in a relationship. It seemed like so long ago. She hadn't spoken to her ex, John in more than two years. Their break up wasn't pleasant at all. The names he called her during their last fight were hurtful. He'd been upset because she was working late hours and had forgotten about an after five event that his firm was throwing him for making partner.

She had gotten home at around midnight and he was sitting in the dark in his tux on her living room couch. They'd exchanged keys months before but he startled her when he called out her name. She turned on the table lamp and looked at him wondering why he was all dressed up when it finally hit her what day it was. "Good Lord John I......." He held up his hand to stop her before she could continue. "You know Marie, I've known for some time that I was second to your business. I've tried to understand that as a business owner you have to put in long hours and sacrifice a lot. But you of all people knew how important this was to me" he said. The hurt in his eyes tore at her heart but she held her ground. "John, I was balancing the books and unpacking the new orders that came in today. I didn't even notice the time." She said matter-of-factly and without emotion. "Why didn't you remind me that we had a party to go to?" she said. "You don't get it do you? he said getting up from the chair. "This is all that I've been talking about for the last three weeks. You hired a staff to do those things for you Marie. Let them do what they were hired to do. You've turned into this ice princess, this shell of a woman. You only think of yourself. You haven't been there for me Marie, admit it." He said as he stood shaking his head. "Even when we are making love you are somewhere else. You are a self-centered, selfish individual. I cannot do this anymore. You probably won't even notice that I'm gone" he said as he walked to the door and placed her key on the entry table. She followed him wanting somehow to correct things. "I feel so sorry for you Marie. You've become so driven and cold that you don't even realize the most important things in life. To what expense are you willing to succeed...huh, Marie?" He stood so close to her she could smell the spearmint on his breath. "This so-called relationship is for the birds. I have too much to offer a woman to feel like I have to beg for you to touch me, or take the time to remember one of the most important days of my life." He threw up his hands in finality and walked to the door. "I wish you luck with the book store but please, don't call me anymore." And he was gone. He never once called or stopped by after that night. She read a few months later that he'd taken on a big racketeering case involving a high powered business man. He was posing in the article with a gorgeous woman on his arm. He looked very happy, she was almost sorry to say. He'd moved on. For a long time she remained cold and very bitter. Despising all men she came in contact with. Her store flourished and she surrounded herself with her friends and work. She hadn't dated seriously or even given thought to a committed relationship until Parnell.

Chapter 16
Promises, promises...

It's obvious she knows about us Erik. What the hell are you waiting for? She saw me leaving your house for goodness sakes" Pam said. Erik sat on the end of the bed with his face in his hands. "Calm down baby. I just need a little more time. What's the big rush anyway? Why all of a sudden you are demanding that I leave Gayle?" He got up to gather his things. "You are so sorry Erik." She said standing to face him. "When we started this whole thing, you told me that you were about to leave her and get a condo. You said that you all were putting the final touches on your separation. You told me that she was staying at her moms. Why the hell do you think I would come over to your house and have sex in your bed if I didn't think that woman was living somewhere else?" Pam snatched his shirt from his hands and threw it on the floor. "Now I find out that you two are living under the same roof! If looks could kill, I'd be dead ten times over. The other day she saw me leaving your home Erik. She has to know something is up." Pam began to cry. "I can't work with you every day and spend time with you when you are still with your wife. You're making me feel like I'm some two dollar tramp that you care nothing for." she flopped down on the bed and buried her face in the pillow crying.

Erik had to think of something. He sat on the edge of the bed and rubbed her back. "Listen baby, Gayle is not stable. She's always talking about ending it if we can't be together." He said trying to get her to turn over and look at him. "She doesn't have a lot of family to turn to and she's always depended on me." Pam shrugged him off and sat up hitting him with her fists in his chest. "What about me Erik? I know you don't expect me to wait in the wings while you lay with your wife every night. You've lost sight of reality if you do." She got up and went to the bedroom window. Erik tried to get

41

her to calm down. He was supposed to meet Gayle at the restaurant in an hour. "I totally understand where you're coming from baby." He turned her around to face him. "I want us to be together Pam but this is not an overnight thing. You have to trust me on this" he said. She wanted to believe him but she wanted him now. "Erik, if you want to be with me then you *would want* to make a decision. This pretending is getting old fast." Pam went into the bathroom and started the shower. Erik quickly got dressed and was ready to leave by the time she finished in the bathroom. "Listen baby, I'm going to meet a couple of the guys for a drink. I'll give you a call a little later or I'll see you in the office tomorrow." He slowly kissed her and moved her hair out of her face. Pam couldn't look him in the eye. "Whatever Erik. You just remember what I said. I'm not going to wait forever." she said. He kissed her once more and left before she could say anything else.

"You are fifteen minutes late Erik. I was just about to leave. Where the hell were you? I must've called your cell ten times" a frustrated Gayle said. "I got held up at work Gayle. What would you have me do, walk out of a meeting?" Erik said taking a seat at the table. "You could've called to tell me you'd be late. Is that too much to ask?" Gayle looked at him suspiciously. "Can we not argue for once Gayle. Is it possible to have a nice meal without all the bitching?" Erik tried to turn the tables. Gayle looked right through him. She could smell another woman on him. He must think she's two kinds of fool 'cause he comes at her with some of the stupidest excuses. What he didn't know was that she called his office during lunch and his secretary told her that he'd left for the day. She was sure he told his secretary to say he was in meetings but Kathy liked Gayle. "You look tired baby, long day at work?" Gayle asked putting her napkin in her lap. "Yeah, they've been getting their money's worth outta me these days. How was your day?" he asked buttering his bread as the waiter approached. "Just fine babe. Oh, I ordered your usual for you. I hope that's OK" Gayle said. "Thanks baby, I'm starving." He didn't even look up as the waiter placed their food on the table and left them to their meals. She watched him wolf down his food like he hadn't eaten in days. Gayle tried to remember what attracted her to Erik years ago. She was sure now it was the chase. She had to have him. Around the old neighborhood he had every woman he wanted but he'd chosen her to be his wife. At first that made her proud. Now she felt like their marriage was doomed from the very start.

Erik had never been a one woman man. His father was the same way. His mom was always carting them off to find their daddy at all times of the day and night. She'd fight any woman that stood between her and her man, too. There were many times when Gayle's mom would bring Erik and his two brothers into their home while his parents duked it out in the street. After their make-up session, they'd walk hand in hand down the street to Gayle's house to retrieve their children. During these times Gayle never paid any attention to Erik or his brothers. They'd all watch television or play SORRY until their parents came for them. It wasn't until they were teenagers that Gayle realized how fine Erik was. Then it was on. She chased away every girl that came looking for him. He'd promised he loved only her and that the others meant nothing to him. He'd promised that he would take care of her and never hurt her. Now she sat in disgust as she watched him eat. She loved him so much she hated him. Even after he slept with her friend weeks before they were to be married, she still held out hope. He'd promised….

Gayle hadn't been feeling well all day that day. The planning of the wedding was getting the best of her. Her nerves were on edge all of the time and she couldn't focus at work. She told her boss that she would be leaving a half day so that she could go home and take a nap before the busy weekend that lay ahead. She had her final fitting on Saturday morning, a meeting with the caterers at noon and then later that evening, she and Erik were to meet for dinner and a movie. Erik's condo was maybe ten minutes from her job thankfully. They each had keys to each other's places for almost a year now. She couldn't wait to take everything off and climb into his bed for some much needed rest. The wedding was supposed to be small but had grown into a guest list of over 200. It was starting to cost a small fortune and she was feeling so overwhelmed with it all.

When she pulled into the lot she noticed Erik's car. Good, she thought. Maybe they could nap together. When she entered she immediately knew something was wrong. Erik's clothes were strewn all over the living room and there were some sandals in the hallway that she knew weren't hers. Gayle took off her earrings and shoes cause she knew there would be some ass whooping going on if what she thought was happening was really happening. When she got to the bedroom she put her ear to the door but didn't hear anything. She tip toed back out through the living room and into the spare room on the other side of the condo. She pulled her cell phone out of her purse and called Erik's cell. He picked up on the third ring. "Hey baby, I was just thinking about you" he said. "What's going on sweetie" she asked. "Nothing much, what time are you getting off today" he asked. "I actually got off a little early today. I'm on my way over to your place to grab some things and then Shelly and I are going to have lunch. Why?" she asked. "Oh I was just wondering. Look I gotta run. I'll talk to you later. Love ya" he said and hung up. Gayle walked back across the living room and up to the bedroom door. Erik was telling the woman to get up. They were frantically gathering up their things and he was yelling at her to hurry because I was on my way. She was helping him to make the bed when Gayle opened the door to the bedroom. With all the hurry they didn't see here standing there. Gayle almost became physically ill when she saw Shelly, her supposed friend, standing there butt ass naked making Erik's bed.

Before either of them knew what was coming Gayle was on her ass. She yelled for dear life as she got the crap beat out of her. All the while, Gayle was crying and cussing like a sailor. Erik was looking like a deer caught in headlights. Eventually, he grabbed Gayle and said to stop because she was killing her. "Stop it Gayle. Stop it!" he said. Shelly looked like she'd gone 12 rounds with Tyson when Gayle backed up off of her. Then it was Erik's turn. Gayle took the five pound weights that he used to work out with and threw them at his head. One connected and he hit the floor holding his head. As the knot grew on the side of his head Shelly tried to regain her composure and began to cry and try to explain. Gayle told her that it would be in her best interest to get out of her sight before she tossed her ass out of the window. She quickly grabbed her things and exited the room. Erik told Gayle that she'd taken advantage of him. He said that he came home for lunch and she must've followed him.

She knocked on the door and said that she wanted to borrow a pair of Gayle's shoes and the purse that matched. He said that when he came into the bedroom to see if she'd found everything; she was lying on the bed naked with her legs spread open. He pleaded and begged for forgiveness. He said that he was so scared and nervous about the wedding that he was weak.

Gayle went to the phone and called the police and told them that her fiancé had been beaten and stabbed and could somebody come quickly and then she hung up. Erik looked confused until he saw Gayle going to the kitchen. "Gayle, what are you doing baby? Let's talk about this" he said following her. She proceeded to get the largest knife that he had out of the drawer and went after him with it. By the time the police knocked on the door, Erik was pleading with them to help him. He was treated at Howard University for minor stab wounds and a slight concussion. He never pressed charges and spent two days in the hospital. He spent the remaining week and a half sending flowers, wining and dining her and kissing her ass until finally he was forgiven. That following Saturday Gayle was a beautiful bride walking down the aisle. He was looking handsome as ever in his Dior tux with just a hint of a fading black eye. And it's been nothing but marital bliss ever since.

Chapter 17
The Game

Michelle waited outside for Alyssa to come out of dance practice. After about ten minutes, she walked out of the studio with a handsome gentleman that looked to be in his early twenties. They spoke for a few minutes and he walked her to the car. "Hello, I'm Terrell Jones. I'll be instructing Alyssa and her team from now on" he said as he reached through the window and shook Michelle's hand. "It's very nice to meet you Terrell. How was she today?" Michelle asked as Alyssa got in the passenger side. "She was fantastic as always" he said looking pass Michelle to give Alyssa a comical look. Alyssa blushed and smiled as she buckled up. "Well, I look forward to seeing you at the recital Terrell" I said. Again, he looked pass Michelle and said his goodbye's to Alyssa.

"He seems nice." I said looking over at Alyssa as I pulled out of the parking lot. "Yeah, he's really cool Mom." Alyssa turned to look at me. "All of the girls think he's great. He's done Broadway and everything! He promised that he'd take us to New York to see a musical soon!" Alyssa raved. Michelle pulled out of the lot and peeked over at Alyssa gushing. "How old is Terrell, Lyssie? He looks so young to have so much experience." "He's 27. Did I tell you that he studied in Paris for two years?" Alyssa said. "No you didn't, honey" Michelle said. Michelle didn't like Alyssa's infatuation with this Terrell character. The way he looked at Alyssa made Michelle cringe inside. He didn't look at her like a teacher would a student. It was almost like a chemistry or something. She was probably overreacting. What would a man want with a 13 year old child anyway?

"You look nice today sweetie" Anthony said to Alyssa. "Mom had to run out for a few so I'll take you to dance rehearsal today." "OK

Daddy. Just let me grab my things and I'll be all set." She ran to her room and Anthony noticed how tight her blouse was. In the car Anthony tried to find an easy way to mention that her clothes were a little too fitting for a pre-teen. "Alyssa, where did you get that blouse? It's really nice but it seems to be a little tight. Are you comfortable in it?" Anthony said trying not to come across too overprotective. Alyssa rolled he eyes and said, "Yes Daddy, I'm fine. This is what everyone is wearing. Terrell bought them for us. We all have the same blouse but in different colors." She said while adjusting her clothes and looking at herself in the visor mirror. Anthony could not believe what he was hearing. "Are you telling me that your instructor bought you this?" Anthony turned in his seat to fully face her. Alyssa seemed to shy away a little. "Dad, you don't understand. He's really nice. He got us these shirts so that we could all dress alike when we go to the dance recital after our rehearsal. They sat in silence for a few minutes after Anthony parked in the dance centers lot. "Look Alyssa, I'm sure his intentions were good but you know better than to accept things from anyone. Does your Mom even know about this?" he wanted to know. "No she doesn't." she said. Alyssa looked like she could spit nails. "I didn't tell her because I knew that she would overreact like you are Daddy. We are supposed to be Christians and the first thing you all do is jump to conclusions. I am so over this." Alyssa started to gather her things. Anthony started to think maybe he'd over reacted. "Wait a minute young lady." Anthony reached over and grabbed her arm. "No one is judging anyone Alyssa. And don't talk to me like I'm one of your friends." He softened his stance a little and pulled her close to him. "It's my job to look for things that you might not see Lyssie. Now, tell Terrell thank you for the kind gesture but in the future he should save the purchase of all things concerning you to your parents." He hugged her tight and then reached over her to open the passenger door. She kissed him on the cheek and added her two cents before she hopped out of the truck. "You are such a tyrant Daddy. You want me to stay a little girl forever. You'll be moving next door to me and my hubby so that you can keep an eye on me when I'm grown and gone." She stuck out her tongue and blew him another kiss and she ran inside. "What's so wrong with that?" he said to himself as he made a mental note to pull this Terrell dude aside and have a little chit chat with him about all of this niceness he was spreading around.

Chapter 18
Drowning

Gayle woke up to Erik's hand around her waist and something else pressing against her back. She thought to herself, *lord please help me not to succumb to him yet again.* She tried to gently slide from under him and he held on even tighter. He felt so good she really didn't want to get up but she had an early meeting this morning that she need to prepare for. "I have to use the bathroom Erik." she whispered. "Hurry back" he says and nudged her one more time with the little soldier for good measure. Gayle went to the bathroom and tried to get herself together. She had been trying to hold out until she decided if his cheating ways had come to a halt or if he was stringing her along for the umpteenth time. After their talk earlier this week he'd said that he knew she deserved better than him. He told her that even though he has a scandalous past, she is the only one for him. Deep down Gayle knew that Erik loved her. She could see it in his eyes. Maybe he has some kind of sickness or something. Eric Benet confessed to Halle that he had a sexual ailment, maybe her husband needed to talk to someone. What was she thinking, he'd never agree to that. That machismo attitude would kick in the moment she broached the subject.

She flushed and started the shower. Hopefully, Erik would get the hint that she wasn't coming back to bed. When she heard the door to the bathroom open, she knew he had another agenda. Erik slid the shower door open and joined Gayle. "What happened baby? I thought you were coming back to bed" he said taking the cloth that she was lathering. "I forgot I have a meeting this morning and I can't be late." Gayle said as she tried not to make eye contact with him. Gayle turned her back to him and let the water run on her face. Erik started to bathe her. Gayle placed both of her hands on the shower wall. He gently washed her and took his time massaging her shoulders and her most sensuous areas. She moaned involuntarily. It had been over two weeks since they made love and he knew just where to touch her. He turned her to face him and whispered that he'd never hurt her again. He just wanted to feel her. He needed to feel her. It was on from there.

Gayle hated to admit it but she absolutely loved their sexual escapades. There was always guilt afterwards because she knew he wasn't faithful to their marriage. This drove Gayle crazy. Afterwards they lay spent on the chair breathing like they had been in a foot race. Gayle glanced at the clock and it was 7:45 AM. "Good grief!" she yelled and sprinted back into the bathroom to wash herself again. "My meeting is at 8:30 Erik. I told you I couldn't be late. Press over the suit that's hanging on the door please. That's the least you could do" she said trying to get her unruly hair to cooperate. Erik smiled and started for the laundry room still naked. "No problem baby" he said leaving the room. "I'll make you some toast and coffee to go too." He grinned to himself. "Don't be so uptight. You'll make the meeting in time" he said as we left to press over her suit.

Gayle cursed herself the entire drive into work. "I do it every time" she said hitting the wheel. "It never fails. I must be the looniest woman in the metropolitan area." She had to smile though. He put that thing on her this morning. Whew! You would've thought she was seizing she climaxed so hard. Lord help her. That man would be her downfall. She made it to the office with ten minutes to prepare. By 8:30 on the nose, she was seated in the board room prepared to meet with the client. As they entered, her cell indicated that she had a text message. It read: The cowboy will be saddled up and ready for a second ride when she got home that evening. Her clients thought that wide grin was for them as she got up to greet them. What a way to start the morning.

Chapter 19
Dressing it Up

Faye applied the second layer of foundation to cover up the bruise on her left cheek. The previous evening she'd made the mistake of asking Calvin why he never brought his cell phone into the house. He always left it in his car. They'd been in bed and he said that he had to go to the car to get a number out of his cell phone. She asked why he always left it in the car anyway? "Do you have something to hide?" She'd asked in a joking sort of way. She meant it to sound like she was kidding but it did seem suspect. His hand came out of nowhere. He slapped her open handed across the face so hard she thought she saw stars. He didn't say anything. He just got up and slipped on his shorts and a shirt and went out to his car. He came back twenty minutes later and asked her what they were eating for dinner.

As Faye looked in the mirror she knew there was no way her friends wouldn't notice the discoloration on her face. She had to be at Michelle's house for Michael's fourth birthday party at two o'clock. Michelle's children loved their Auntie Faye and would not understand her not being there. "Oh well, this will have to do" she said adding finishing touches to her makeup. Calvin was sitting in the recliner when she came out of the bathroom. She sat on the sofa and started wrapping Michael's truck that he'd told her he wanted seven times in the last few days. She'd gone to two Toys R Us stores trying to find it. It had all of the sound effects plus a remote control. She couldn't wait to see his face when he opened it.

She could tell Calvin was in a bad mood. He hadn't spoken more than three words to her all morning. "Where did you say you were going again" he asked. "I told you that my nephew's birthday is

51

today and Michelle and Anthony are having a party at their house. Would you like to come with me baby?" Faye put the wrapping aside and went over and sat on his lap. "It's going to be so nice. Marie and Gayle's significant others will be there too so you'll have some other guys there to talk to." Faye really didn't want him to come and spoil the mood but she knew if she didn't ask he'd be angry. Calvin continued to look at TV. "No thanks." He said. "I have a lot of stuff to do today. By the way, I won't be around for a few days. My job is sending me on travel. I leave Monday morning" he said nonchalantly. Faye stood and smoothed out her clothes. What the hell was this all about? She hadn't told him but after some snooping she found out that he really was the cleaning person at the company and not a partner like he'd told her earlier on. She couldn't figure out why he lied to her. "Why hadn't you mentioned this before? Today is Saturday and we'll only have Sunday to be together before you leave. How long will you be gone anyway?" He was such a bad liar. "Where exactly are you going?" Faye wanted to know. He moved her to the side with his leg so that he could change the channel. "I said I'll be gone for a few days. Don't be asking me no whole bunch of questions either" he said scowling at her. "I got some business that I have to handle in Florida and then in Atlanta. It may take a couple of days or it may take longer. You should be happy. This will give you some time to spend with your nosey ass girlfriends. I know they been all up in our business too." He used the remote to turn the channel on the TV. "You always whispering on the phone with them hags about this and that. Don't think I haven't noticed, alright."

He finally slammed the remote on the table and got up and went into the kitchen. He came back out with a beer and pretzels. Faye had sat back on the sofa to finish wrapping the gift. She did not want to get into it with him. It was as if he wanted to sever every connection that she had with everyone but him. "Look Faye, I don't want to argue right before I leave. How long are you going to be over there today?" he asked as he walked over to the sofa and stood in front of her. "I'm not sure. Why, do you want to take me out somewhere?" she said getting her hopes up. "Maybe we can go to a nice restaurant for dinner or something" she said rising to stand in front of him. She wrapped her arms around his muscular frame and he hugged her.

"Do you really have to go to that party baby? He started rubbing her back and squeezing her behind. "I mean can't you take the gift over there after I leave for my trip? I really want to spend some time with you before I leave." She stepped back and looked at him. She couldn't believe he was doing this. "I have to go Calvin. This is very important to Michael. We have a very special relationship. He would be crushed if I didn't come." She started to gather her things and grabbed her purse.

Calvin had made his way back to the recliner with a disgusted look on his face. "Well it's obvious that they are more important than me, so go ahead." He waved her off as she bent down to kiss him. "You just want to go over there and put on a show for them uppity friends of yours. I won't be here when you get back." He said matter-of-factly. Faye turned just as she reached the door. "Where are you going Calvin?" she hoped she didn't look too desperate. "I told you I have some things to take care of. Bye, I thought you were gone" he said dismissively. "You don't want to be late." He got up and went upstairs to the bedroom and left her at the door looking torn. She knew she would never be forgiven if she didn't go to the party. "OK baby. I'm leaving. I'll give you a call when I get back. Calvin…. Calvin?" He didn't respond. She started for the bedroom and then decided against it. She was already running late. She turned and left the house. She sat in the car for ten minutes wondering if she should go back and talk to him. After checking her make-up in the rear view mirror she saw the reminder of last night and knew that if she went back, she'd never make the party that afternoon. She started the car and left with only a few minutes to spare.

Chapter 20
Cuttin the Rug

"Anthony, you should be leaving to get the cake baby. Why are you still sitting down?" Michelle fussed as she finally finished cleaning and setting the party table. "Honey, there are only a few of Michael's classmates coming over. You've spit shined the entire house like the president is dropping by for a visit" Anthony teased. "Hush man and go get my baby's cake please! Everyone will be here in an hour. I want everything to be perfect" Michelle said. Anthony finally left to get the Spider Man cake that Michael *had* to have. "Alyssa, have you finished stuffing the party bags?" Michelle asked as she was on her way up to wake Michael from his nap. AJ was in the dining room blowing up the last of the balloons. "Yep, it's done Mom. They're on the table in the kitchen. Tell the runt that he'd better save his big sister one or I'm keeping the gift that I got for him." Alyssa slapped AJ on the head as she ran past her Mom to go up to her room. "Mom, please tell her keep her paws off of me!" AJ yelled in his sister's direction. "Lyssie, please keep your paws off of your brother. AJ, take the balloons to the basement and scatter them around." Michelle yelled over her shoulder as she entered Michael's room.

Marie walked into the house and she could hear the music coming from the basement. She popped her fingers as she put the gift next to the various others on the gift table near the basement door. Parnell was still parking the car and she wanted to wait for him before going down. He walked in hand in hand with Faye. "Hey lady!" Faye yelled as she caught sight of Marie with her hand in the chip bowl. They hugged and held hands as they gave each other a once over. "Look at this fine specimen I found outside" Faye said walking back over to Parnell. "He said that he didn't have a date for the party so I figured we could make the best of the situation."

Marie rolled her eyes and snatched Parnell's hand. "This one belongs to me Missy. Parnell, what have I told you about talking to strangers?" Marie said looking Faye up and down. Parnell laughed at them and took in the house. "They have a beautiful home. Michelle is a superb decorator." Marie and Faye smiled at each other. "Yes baby, Michelle could make a shack look like a penthouse. I told her she missed her calling." Marie said as they all made their way down to the basement.

"I thought I saw Gayle's car outside." Faye said. She must be downstairs. They all went down stairs to a bunch of kids playing pin the tail on the donkey. Erik and Anthony were helping the kids play the game. Michelle was adjusting Michael's clothes when he caught sight of Faye. He broke away from Michelle and ran past Marie and Parnell and leapt into her arms. "Auntie Faye, what took you so long? My mom says that you're always late but I knew you'd be here." He kissed the bruised side of her face and she squinted a little. "You knew I'd be here honey bunny!" she said smooching him and tickling his tummy at the same time. She made a silly face at Michelle as she put him down. Michael finally decided to make his rounds and gave Marie a kiss on the cheek and shook hands with Parnell. "Are you my uncle now Parnell?" Michael wanted to know. Marie turned two shades of red and patted Michael on the bottom. "Auntie Marie and Parnell are good friend's baby" Marie said. Parnell thought the whole scene was too funny. He chuckled as he placed a fifty dollar bill in Michael's hand. "Happy birthday lil man" he said. "Michael's eyes nearly bugged out of his head and he ran to his mom. "Mommy, Uncle Parnell gave me fifty whole dollars! I'm going to buy some new trucks and take Auntie Faye out to dinner! Thanks Uncle Parnell." He said. Gayle put her hands on her hips as she came out of the bathroom. "What about me mister?" she wanted to know. "You promised me you'd take me to a movie with your birthday money. Traitor!" she laughed as she hugged Faye and kissed Marie on the cheek. "I'm gonna take you both out Auntie Gayle. I'm rich now!" he said and went to show his friends.

Gayle noticed that Faye's face looked kind of over made up. Faye never wore a lot of makeup. She didn't have to. Faye was a natural beauty. She went over and sat next to her on the couch. "Are you in the running for a drag queen look-a-like or something? Why do you have so much foundation on?" Gayle wanted to know. Faye bumped shoulders with Gayle playfully and commented "It's my honey bunny's birthday and I wanted to look pretty" she said patting her face. She could feel Gayle's eyes staring at her. "Did I overdo it?" Faye asked nervously. Upon closer look Gayle could tell that there was a mark on her cheek. Gayle got up and went over to Michelle at the punch bowl. "Hey you, Faye and I are going to make a store run. I am out of batteries for my camera and I have to have my own pictures of the little man on his birthday. We'll be back in a few OK?" Michelle gave her a quizzical look. Gayle knew that Michelle could take stock in batteries they had so many. With two boys, most of their toys took batteries so Anthony kept a supply in the garage. She and Gayle made eye contact and she hunched her shoulders and said, "Hurry back, we're going to sing happy birthday in a little while. I have to get these sugar hyped children back to their parents before I go crazy."

Gayle went over and kissed Erik on the cheek and told him she'd be back in a few. She grabbed both of Faye's hands and pulled her up from the sofa. "Come go with me to the store chickadee." Gayle had a way of getting Faye to tell her anything. "What are you going to get from the store?" Faye wanted to know. She knew Gayle had something up her sleeve. "Just come on girl. Hurry up before Michael sees you." They hurried up the stairs as Michael pinned the tail on the donkey's nose.

Chapter 21
Fight the Fight

"All right Gayle, why did we have to leave the party?" Faye asked as they pulled out of the driveway. Gayle said nothing for a while. Then she turned off the radio and asked Faye, "How long have we known each other?" Gayle asked looking at her and touching the side of her face that was bruised. "Since forever" Faye said looking down at the floor. Gayle looked straight ahead as she drove out of the cul-de-sac. "You have always been more of a sister than a friend Faye. I know that you and Michelle have always been very close but you and I share a connection of sorts right?" Faye nodded in agreement. Faye could feel herself weakening. Maybe Gayle would understand. She could sure use someone to talk to. This relationship seemed to be draining her. She hadn't mentioned to anyone that she had to go to the emergency room two weeks ago because Calvin *accidentally* pushed her down the stairs after she'd been on the phone with them too long. Gayle continued, "We usually know when something is wrong with one of us. Michelle would've noticed too but she's been caught up with the party today, and Marie has cupids bow stuck up her butt so she hasn't noticed anyone but Parnell. But I could tell the moment I saw you Faye." Gayle reached over and touched Faye's hand. "Now, tell your sister what's up or you'll have to walk back to the house." Faye looked out of the window as tears slowly made their way down her cheeks.

She shook her head in disbelief that this was happening to her. You would think a well-educated woman wouldn't get herself in these predicaments. "I don't know what happened Gayle. It's like I'm a walking sign that says *use me*, or *walk over me* that only men can see." Faye said exasperated. She turned towards Gayle tucking one leg under the other. "In the beginning, Calvin was great. Now, I can't do anything right." Faye buried her face in her hands and had a much needed cry. Gayle pulled over and held her until her sobs subsided. "You have such a loving heart Faye" Gayle said. "Some men prey on that. You've done nothing but love that man. He should be doing all that he can to stay in your good graces." Gayle brushed back Faye's short curly hair and lifted her chin. "Did he do this to your face sweetie?" Gayle asked while taking a napkin and cleaning the mascara and foundation that was making its way down Faye's face onto her blouse.

"I always push, Gayle. Do you think I fall in love too quickly?" Faye looked at herself in the mirror and searched around in her purse for her makeup kit. "Yuck, I look like a rabid raccoon." Gayle turned to face Faye. "Faye, when you fall in love you should not be rewarded for giving your heart to someone by getting a slap in the face, or a punch in the gut. You haven't realized your worth. You are college educated, you're a home owner, and you are also smarter than most people I know. To top it off, you make crazy loot at that snooty accounting firm you're with." They both smiled through their tears. "Even with all of that, you are kind and caring and those are qualities that are a rare commodity these days. A man should feel privileged to be in your presence let alone in love with you. Sweetie, you love so hard that you don't realize you lose yourself." Gayle turned in her seat and rested her head on the headrest. "Faye, Calvin doesn't deserve you." Faye tried to interrupt but Gayle shushed her. "Stop making excuses for his worthless ass." Gayle set up and was ready to give attitude. "You don't have the man's home number, Faye." Gayle went down the list. "You've never been to his residence. Hell, you don't even know what he does for a living. Be thankful that he's shown his true colors now as opposed to farther down the road when you've invested years into him. For all you know, he has a wife and six crumb snatchers living on the other side of town." They both shared a laugh at the thought.

They sat quietly for a while. Faye felt a since of relief. Gayle's pep talks could motivate anyone. Finally Gayle said, "I have some nerve don't I?" she said looking over at her friend. "My husband is a lying, cheating, snake in the grass and I love him so much I can't stand it. Who the hell am I to give you advice?" Gayle threw up her hands and laid her head on the head rest again. Faye grabbed her hand. It was her turn to comfort her friend. "The difference is Erik loves you Gayle. He always has. He just has to learn that his manhood isn't measured by the length of his penis." Faye said. They both turned and looked at each other and burst into laughter. They laughed so hard they ruined their now repaired makeup. Passersby drove by looking at them as if they'd lost their minds. After a few minutes they gathered themselves and Gayle started her car. They headed back to the party that was nearing an end.

By the time they arrived, Michelle was out front saying her goodbye's to Michael's friends and their parents. As Michelle, waved at the last of the cars to leave, Faye and Gayle had gotten out of the car and was making their way up the walkway. "Where have you cows been? Some help you all were." Michelle said with her hands on her hips. Gayle looked at her and thought Michelle was so lucky. She is such a great mommy and wife. She was meant to do this kind of stuff. Gayle had always wanted children but it never happened. Michelle looked behind her to make sure Marie wasn't listening. "Yall know darn well Marie and children don't mix. A little boy was sitting beside her at the table and made the mistake of putting his sticky hand on her pants. You would've thought the child had cooties she acted out so badly." Michelle covered her mouth to avoid laughing so loud. "Parnell has a kind soul to put up with that crazy lady." Michelle chatted away until she realized that her two friends looked like they had just come from a sappy movie or something.

She looked closer at Faye and noticed her face. "What the......" Michelle started as she touched Faye's face. "I've already done the sister talk and she knows what she has to do." Gayle said. "Did you give her good advice Gee Gee or did you tell her to cut someone?" Michelle wanted to know. Gayle nudged Michelle with her hip and they all smiled and made their way inside. "I'm sorry I didn't notice sooner baby girl." Michelle said linking her arm in Faye's. "I've been going crazy between getting the party ready, getting Lyssie ready for her recital, and doing the books for Anthony that I've been a neglectful friend." Just then Marie was coming up with the last of the food trays. She placed them in the dish washer and joined her crew in the foyer. "Did I miss something" she said. Faye and Gayle giggled as they looked at the handprint on Marie's pants and what looked like little pieces of confetti caught in her long hair. "What are you all laughing at?" Marie eyed both of them suspiciously. "Nothing cutie pie" Faye said picking the confetti out of Marie's hair. After they put the food away, they all sat for a while before Parnell said that he should be calling it a night since he had a long drive ahead of him. Anthony and Michelle saw them off and then tidied up more in the kitchen.

"Are you coming up to bed baby?" Anthony asked folding the dish towel and placing it on the counter. "I'll help you clean the basement in the morning." He said. Michelle smiled and playfully patted his behind. "You go on up, love. I'll be there in a minute. I just want to lock up and check downstairs once more." Anthony gratefully retreated upstairs as Michelle cut off lights, started the dishwasher and set the alarm.

When she reached the top of the stairs, she noticed a dim light under Alyssa's door. Michelle quietly opened the door and Alyssa was at her computer with her back to Michelle. It looked as if she was chatting online. Alyssa was so into the conversation that she hadn't heard Michelle walking towards her. Michelle was able to read a few lines from someone saying "you looked good enough to eat" and something about "when are you going to let me see it." Alyssa spun around blocking the monitor. "Mommy, why didn't you say something?" Alyssa asked while reaching over and clicking on her screen saver. "You nearly gave me a heart attack. Is the runt in bed yet?" Alyssa asked fiddling nervously. Michelle inched closer to Alyssa. "Yes baby, your dad put him in bed over an hour ago. What were you doing?" Michelle tried to read her face. Her children were horrible liars. "I was just telling Angie about the new steps we learned today in practice. She had a doctor's appointment and didn't make practice today." Alyssa said trying to sound convincing.

Michelle knew what she saw and knew Lyssie wasn't talking to Angie at all. "How is Angie doing? Is everything OK with her?" Michelle asked to see just how far Alyssa would go with this. "She's fine mom. Just a check-up or something." Alyssa smiled and got up from her chair and flopped down on her bed. She wanted to divert her mom's attention away from the computer. "It's getting late Lyssie. You know the computer should be off after eight. Get ready for bed, baby." Michelle bent to kiss Alyssa and paused to take a long look at her oldest child. Her daughter seemed to be growing up overnight. Alyssa was such a beautiful girl. What was her baby getting in to? "Have a great night sweetie. Mommy, loves ya kiddo." Michelle said kissing Alyssa. "I love you much, lady." Alyssa said as they rubbed noses like they've always done since Alyssa could remember. Michelle tucked her oldest in to bed. She made her rounds and checked her boys as she did every night. AJ was fast asleep with the remote in his hand. Michael had Elmo safely tucked in his arm and his stuffed dinosaur on the other side of him. As Michelle slid under the covers beside a snoring Anthony, she thought of what she'd read on Lyssie's computer and said a silent prayer. "God please protect my baby. She is a good girl. Keep her from all hurt, harm or danger. And don't make me have to kill someone for hurting her. In Jesus' name, Amen." It was a long night for Michelle. Anthony would hit the roof if he found out. Was she making a big deal out of nothing? Lyssie never gave them any problems before. She tossed and turned the entire night.

Chapter 22
Always a Bride's Maid…

"I love you Marie. I've loved you from the moment we met. You are a remarkable woman. I'm lucky someone hasn't scooped you up yet." Parnell held her close and rubbed her back as they lay side by side in his bed. They'd been seeing each other for a while now and Marie was a little scared to admit that she'd fallen in love with him too. She snuggled deeper into his arms. "Tell me, where do we go from here? I'm getting too old to play the dating game." Parnell said. Marie knew this was coming. She'd had her guard up for so long that she didn't know how to handle this. Parnell was always so attentive to her. He seemed to put her first in everything they did together. The last thing she wanted was to lose him but she had to be sure he was the one. "I love what we have Parnell" Marie said while slipping from his strong arms and laying on her back. "I just want us to be sure this is what we both want."

Parnell sat up in the bed and looked at her in disbelief. "I know exactly what I want, Marie. I've been clear on that from the beginning." He got up from the bed and slipped on his pants. "The question is, what do you want? When are you going to let me in and stop trying to conceal what you really feel?" He came around to her side of the bed. She'd sat up and put on her bath robe. She tried her best not to look at the hurt in his eyes. This is not going the way she'd planned, she thought. Parnell grabbed her by both shoulders and slowly pulled her up so they were standing face to face. "I'm not in the habit of begging any woman to be with me, Marie. This will not be the day that I start. I suggest you evaluate this and make a decision. Either you are going to continue to question every good thing that happens in your life or you are going to let me love you." He let go of her and went to the bathroom to shower. Before he closed the door he told her "after we're dressed, I'll drive you back.

I don't think we should see each other again until you've made your decision on where you want this relationship to go." And that was it. He closed the bathroom door and left her to her misery. She hugged herself and cursed her heart. Why couldn't she tell him how much she'd come to love and rely on him.

They drove in silence the entire way. Parnell had a pensive look as though he was deep in thought. Marie wanted to reach over and touch him but was afraid that he would reject her. When they finally pulled in front of her home he didn't even turn off the engine. He looked straight ahead and waited for her to gather her things. "I have a few signings coming up so I'll be on the go for a while. I will email you with my itinerary should you need to contact me. Be well, Marie." He said with finality. She waited for a moment thinking he would reach over and kiss her, or walk her to the door as he'd always done in the past. Instead there was an awkward silence. "Do you know how long you'll be gone?" She asked in a final attempt to start a conversation. "I'm not sure Marie. He said. "I have to clear my head and work will help me keep my mind off of things. I'll call you when I have a chance. Now...I have to get back to the house to finish some last minute things." Parnell said indicating that this conversation was over. Marie's heart sank as she slowly exited the car. As soon as she got to her front door, Parnell pulled away from the sidewalk. She quickly dug into her purse to find her cell phone. She'd call him and make things right. She started to dial and felt like a fool. What would she say? She'd hurt the only man that seemed to love her without cost. With shaking hands, she unlocked her front door and dropped all of her things in the foyer. She made her way to her bedroom and cried like she'd just lost her best friend. She'd done it again. The Ice Princess was destined to be alone in life. She didn't remember falling into a fitful sleep and awoke to find herself still dressed and on top of the covers. She couldn't help but cry again.

Chapter 23
Lights, Camera, Action!

The group practiced their last number. Alyssa was center stage and the other girls surrounded her. The number ended with Alyssa hitting the final note and the girls falling to her feet. The recital was in three months and they had almost perfected the performance. Terrell looked at Alyssa's body in wonderment. She was perfect in every way. She was so supple and sweet, he got excited just looking at her. What attracted him to her was that she wasn't like the others. She had no idea how beautiful she was. He would have her, he thought. The girls were in a group sitting on stage talking amongst themselves as Terrell got up from his seat in the audience and walked to the stairs of the stage. "Alyssa, can I speak with you a moment?" he asked. Using a towel to wipe perspiration from her neck and back, Alyssa got up and took a swig of her bottled water. The others continued in their banter as she went to the stairs and kneeled down to see what he wanted. "You were marvelous as usual today, Lyssie. Do you mind if I call you Lyssie?" he asked. "No, not at all. Thanks for the compliment Terrell, we've been working hard on this recital. There'll be recruiters here from Alvin Ailey and Duke Ellington, so I really want to make a great impression." The other girls started gathering their things in preparation to leave. Alyssa took that as her cue to get ready also. "Alyssa, you are way more talented than the others." He touched her arm to hold her there a moment longer.

"Maybe I could put in a good word for you when the recruiters arrive." Terrell knew he had her. These girls wait a lifetime for an opportunity like this. Alyssa stopped dead in her tracks. "Really Terrell?! That would be great. I mean, do you think they'd listen to you?" Alyssa couldn't believe her luck. Her mom was so wrong about him. "Why wouldn't they take my advice? I mean, I'm one of your instructors. If anybody knows your potential it'd be me, right?" Terrell could feel himself getting excited again. "I could give you some personal training if you'd like. You know, tips on what I've learned in the industry that could help you outshine the others." He said. Alyssa was all ears. "Why don't you stay a while longer? Who's coming to get you today?" Terrell hoped it wasn't her dad. That dude looked like a linebacker. "My mom is coming. I still have half an hour before she gets here though." Alyssa said. Terrell thought this was perfect timing. "Great. We have to start with some new stretching exercises though. We don't want you to strain your muscles." Terrell tried to contain himself. He got up on the stage and moved some of the stage props so they'd have enough room. Alyssa had on a ballerina skirt over her tights and a tank top. Her hair was pulled back in a loose pony tail. Terrell stood behind her and carefully placed his hands on her hips. "You have to bend over. I'll hold your hips to help you with your form." Alyssa felt a little uncomfortable. Why did he have to stand behind her like that. It felt like something was jabbing her near her butt. "Maybe you could do the stretch and I could watch, Terrell. This way I can see what you mean." She said trying unsuccessfully to move from in front of him. She turned to face him and he was standing so close she could feel his breath on her face. Out of nowhere Terrell grabbed the back of her head and shoved his tongue down her throat.

Alyssa pushed him away and wiped her mouth. Nervous tears streamed down her face. "What are you doing Terrell?" Alyssa looked around and no one was there but them. "Didn't you like it Lyssie?" Terrell reached for her hand and brought it to his crotch. "I've seen you dance for me Lyssie. You want this inside of you don't you?" Alyssa snatched away from him and ran over to the opposite side of the stage and grabbed her things. Where in the world was her mom? She made her way down the stairs and started down the center aisle of the auditorium. Terrell yelled after her. "Let this be our secret Lyssie. We wouldn't want those recruiters to think you're the stuck up bitch that the other girls think you are." Alyssa turned around and he was still grabbing at himself. She felt sick to her stomach. "They're my friends, Terrell. They don't think that way about me." He smiled slyly as he watched her. She was so ripe. He should take her right now. "After I tell them how you said you were the best dancer in the recital, they'll think whatever I want them to think." He laughed. "We could settle this now if you'd like. Come on back to the stage and let me make you a woman, Lyssie." Alyssa turned and ran to the doors. She burst through them and ran smack into her mom.

"Alyssa, what's the rush baby?" Michelle said noticing the urgency in her eyes. Alyssa hugged her mom and turned her around so they could leave. "Never mind mom. Let's just go please." Alyssa couldn't get out of there fast enough. Michelle turned back and saw Terrell doing something with the props on stage. She thought she'd get a chance to pick his brain about the conversation that he and Alyssa was having the other night, but Alyssa seemed to be in such a rush. They made their way to the car and Michelle could see that her daughter was really upset about something. "Is everything alright Lyssie? You look like something is the matter." Michelle was starting to get a little worried. They buckled up and started for home. "I'm fine mom. I'm just tired. I want to go home and go to bed. This recital is wearing me out." Alyssa wanted to tell her mom what happened, but she was afraid her mom would take her out of dance. Her chances of getting into a good school would be down the toilet. She would have to handle this herself. Her stomach was doing summersaults. She tilted her seat back and closed her eyes. What was Terrell thinking? Had she done something to lead him on? The look in his eyes terrified her. How could she go to rehearsal on Friday and face him? When they got home she went straight to the bathroom to shower. She felt so dirty. She scrubbed until her skin felt raw. She slipped on baggy sweats and a large t-shirt and lay in bed. This was the worst day of her life.

Chapter 24
Daddy's Girl

Michelle and Anthony lay in bed. Michelle was reading her latest novel and Anthony searched to find something decent to watch on the TV. He finally decided on Hoodlum with Lawrence Fishburne. He was a bad brotha in this movie. As soon as Anthony settled in to watch, Michelle put down her book and turned to him. "Baby, we need to talk." Why did she always need to talk when he wanted to relax? He just wanted to sit back and watch Fishburne take on the mob, maybe get a foot rub a little later on, and then get some much needed rest. As usual, he yielded to Michelle. "What's on your mind, baby?" he asked propping up the pillows beneath his head. He hoped she'd make it quick. He was willing to talk as long as whatever she needed didn't require him to move from this spot. Maybe he'd still get to catch the ending of the movie. "Anthony, something's going on with Alyssa. This Terrell guy is starting to worry me." Michelle proceeded with caution as she watched the expression change on Anthony's face.

"Why don't you tell me exactly what the matter is, Michelle" he sat up on the bed. After his discussion with Alyssa about Terrell buying her the t-shirt, he thought all was well. They'd never had any reason not to trust their daughter before. Michelle searched for the right words to say. "He seems to be coming on a bit too strong. I mean, he seems to be getting a little too close to her." Why did she have to say that? Anthony immediately took this to mean something had happened that Michelle didn't bother to mention to him. He could feel himself getting heated. "Is there something you need to say to me Michelle? Cause all of this tap dancing is starting to get on my nerves." Michelle was starting to get frustrated. Anthony always over-reacted when it came to the kids. Why did everyone call her the overprotective one? "Anthony, it's the way that he looks at her.

67

It makes my skin crawl." Michelle shuddered. "It's like he's lusting after her right in front of me." Anthony ran his hands down his face and flung the covers to the side and got out of bed. Lawrence Fishburne would have to wait. He walked back and forth at the foot of the bed. Michelle almost wished she hadn't said anything. They were probably feeding too much into this. "Are you telling me that this punk is being inappropriate with my baby? Anthony pointed towards the bedroom door. "If he so much as puts his hands on her, I will break his little scrawny ass in two." Michelle set up a little further. "Anthony, be quiet before you wake up the kids. I'm only saying that I get this feeling…." Michelle struggled to get her words right. "….like if given the chance, he'd teach her more than just dance moves."

Michelle grabbed the remote and turned the TV off. She knew they'd be a while. Anthony looked as if he would blow any minute. "When I picked her up from practice she was all flustered and shaken like something had happened, but she wouldn't tell me. She blew it off and said that she wanted to get home." Michelle wondered if she should tell him about the instant message that she'd read. Anthony came and sat next to her on her side of the bed. "Maybe she got into it with one of the other girls." he said. "You know how they are, friends one day and enemies the next." Anthony sounded more like he was trying more to convince himself than Michelle. "I don't think so baby." Michelle said. "All of the girls were gone by the time I got there. Besides, Lyssie always tells me about the spats that they have. She's never kept that a secret. I'm telling you that it's something more." Anthony let go of her hand. "Are you telling me that you were you late getting her Michelle? I mean was she there alone with that little punk?" Anthony could feel a headache coming on. He got up and paced the floor again. "I got there at my normal time, Anthony. Some of the girls were probably in the locker room changing. Let's not place blame here. I'm probably just being overly cautious." The last thing she wanted was to argue. She wanted him to understand that there was something about this guy that wasn't right. "I'm not placing blame Michelle. Maybe I should pick her up from practice for a while." Anthony wanted a little alone time with Terrell. He needed Terrell to see that Alyssa had a dad that didn't mind going upside his head if need be.

"That won't be necessary Anthony. I'm capable of picking up my children. I just think we should keep our eyes and ears open." Her feelings a little hurt, Michelle took extra special care in fixing the covers on the bed. Anthony sensing that he'd upset her went over and gently grabbed her shoulders and embraced her in a much needed hug. "We'll get through this baby. Whatever *this* is, it's nothing we can't handle. Maybe we need to have a heart to heart with Alyssa. You know, explain to her the dangers that are out there." He let go of her and got back into bed. Michelle felt a little better but still couldn't shake the feelings that she was having. Anthony pulled her close to him and she nestled her head on his chest.

"Remember when Lyssie was a little girl" Anthony said remembering how rambunctious Alyssa had been. "She'd befriend all of the new kids in school. She always defended the kids that others made fun of. I don't ever remember a time when she complained about someone not liking her." Anthony laughed a bit. "She never seemed to care." She gets that from her mom ya know?" he said pulling her even closer. "I don't think I'm ready for this Anthony. The boys, the phone calls in the middle of the night, the sneakiness. I just want her to stay a little girl a while longer." Michelle said feeling herself relax. She felt so safe in Anthony's arms. She shut her eyes and welcomed sleep. The last thing she remembered hearing was Anthony reassuring her that Alyssa was a good girl. She would do the right thing when the time came. She prayed that he was right.

Chapter 25
First Time, Shame on you…..

Marie entered her house at around nine in the evening exhausted. She'd stayed at the book store entering some last minute orders and checking the stock. Even though she had an excellent staff, she always made sure she double checked everything from the coffee supply to trash bags. They were expecting a snow storm next week and people always wanted to snuggle up with a good book instead of braving the elements. She wanted to make sure they had enough of the best sellers in stock.

She also needed a diversion since she hadn't spoken with Parnell in over two weeks. His assistant was pleasant enough but she could tell she was covering for him. Marie hadn't had a good night's sleep since their last night together. Lord knows good men are hard enough to find. Why was it so hard to give her heart to one of the most caring and gentlemen she'd ever met? She was always waiting for the other shoe to drop. She tried to contain herself but she must've left at least six messages with Parnell's service. The operator was starting to recognize her voice so she stopped calling.

Marie tidied up the already clean kitchen, brewed herself a cup of peppermint tea and made her way upstairs. She ran extra hot water in the soaking tub so that she could sit for a while before trying to get some much needed rest. She and Alyssa were supposed to have a girl's night but Alyssa cancelled saying she was going to hang out with one of her friends this weekend. It's sad when a 13 year old has more of a social life than her tired old auntie. She got settled in the bath with a book that she was re-reading for the third time when she thought she heard the doorbell. "I know darn well no one is ringing my doorbell at this time of the night." She said. Just when she was sure she was hearing things she heard the doorbell twice more.

"Well I'll be…." Marie said as she put the book down and reached for her bath robe.

She snatched open the door ready to give it to whomever had the ordacity to be at her door ringing like the police. She pulled open the door with such force that she had to readjust her robe. "Faye….what in the hell are you doing out this time of night?" Faye looked disheveled and appeared to be out of breath. She had no coat on and looked like she was about to run over Marie to get in the house. "I'm so sorry to drop in Marie, but can I come in?" Faye said as she brushed pass Marie and went through the foyer into the family room. She flopped onto the sofa and immediately started crying. Marie didn't have time to react. She had to think to close the door and turned to run after Faye. "What is going on Faye? Where is your coat and why are you out in the night like this?" Faye tried to get herself together. Marie grabbed a box of tissues from off of the coffee table and attempted to wipe Faye's face. "I tried Marie. I tried to tell him that we were through. He went crazy! He said that I belong to him." Marie tried to make sense of what Faye was saying through her tears and shortness of breath.

"Calm down sweetie and tell me what happened. Are you hurt? Should I call Michelle and Gayle? They'd know what to do." Marie had to admit that they were better at comforting and solving problems than she was. She attempted to get up from the sofa so that she could make the call when Faye shook her head frantically and pulled her back to the sofa. Faye tried to gather herself so that she could tell Marie what happened. She started telling Marie that after Calvin came back from another one of his disappearing acts she'd asked him if he could come over. She was determined to either get answers from him about their relationship and his whereabouts or she'd tell him it was over. When he got there, he acted as if everything was fine between them and was all over her.

When she started questioning him about why couldn't she have his home number or where exactly was his house, he got this look in his eyes like he could kill her. He told her not to question him and that she needed to get out of his business. He ranted that the problem with women is that they nagged too much. She told him that she only wanted from him the same that he'd gotten from her. That's when it hit the fan. "He grabbed me by my hair and said that if I wanted to know where he lived so badly then he'd show me. He practically dragged me out to his car and told me that if I tried to get out he'd run me over." Faye blew her nose and Marie silently wished she could call Michelle over. She had no idea what to do to help Faye. "Well that explains why you don't have your coat. He's lost his mind dragging you outside like that. Come on…" she said standing. "Let me get you some tea. It'll make you feel a little better." They made their way to the kitchen and Faye sat at the table while Marie busied herself in the refrigerator pulling out sandwich makings, fruit juice and whatever else she could find. Faye blew her nose again and fresh tears made their way down her face.

Marie made her way to the kitchen table balancing a plated tuna sandwich, some bananas and two mugs of chamomile tea. Faye sniffled and asked Marie what was with all of the food. "People usually eat when they're feeling sad right? Well eat up!" Marie said. Marie went back for chips and finally sat down in the chair across from Faye and took a sip of her tea. "If he had you in the car, how'd you get here?" Faye opened the Sun Chips and glared at Marie. "If you'll stop interrupting, I'll tell you!" Marie gave her a pensive look telling her to get on with it. Faye told her that once they were in the car, she tried to calm him down. She kept apologizing and suggesting that they go back to her house and talk it over. He wouldn't say anything to her. She noticed that they seemed to be driving for an awfully long time. It generally took him only 15 minutes max to get to her coming from his *supposed house*.

When she questioned him again as to where they were going, he told her that he refused to live without her. He said that she'd be the last one to tear out his heart. Faye thought he'd lost his mind. He was driving like a mad man and yelling obscenities at the other drivers on the road. When they got stuck in traffic because they'd closed off one of the lanes for construction, Faye was able to manually unlock the door and jump out. Calvin yelled for her to get back in the car before she made him come after her. "If only you could've seen his face Marie. He looked like he could kill me" Faye said shaking her head. "I've been walking for the last two hours. I didn't want to call

Michelle and wake Anthony and the kids, and Gayle has enough on her mind" she started crying again. "What am I going to do? I can't go back home Marie. I have never been so afraid in my life." Marie got up and came around to Faye's side of the table. She held her until her tears subsided. "You can stay here as long as you'd like. We have to call the girls Faye. They'll be furious if we don't."

Chapter 26
Down but Not Out

Gayle had just gotten into a good sleep. She was dreaming that Erik was on TV giving a press briefing professing his love for her. All of the reporters were women that he'd slept with and they started throwing things at him. The women were yelling obscenities at him and their voices started to collide. The voices started to sound like a siren of sorts. Gayle was jarred out of her sleep to the telephone ringing. She peeped at the clock and it read one o'clock AM. Erik never moved as she reached over and grabbed the cordless. "Hello" she asked thinking that some heffa was finally bold enough to call her home for Erik.

"Gayle, it's Marie. Look, we have a slight situation." Gayle got a feeling in the pit of her stomach like someone had died or something. "What is it Marie? Are you OK?" Gayle sat up in bed and threw the covers off of her. Erik was sleeping so deeply that he never heard a thing. "I'm fine. Faye is here and well.....she needs us Gayle. She and Calvin......they, uh..." Gayle could hear the phone switching hands. Faye had snatched the phone from Marie. She could hear Marie fussing at Faye for snatching the phone. Gayle pressed her ear to the phone and said, "Hello Marie? Faye?! Will someone get on the darn phone and tell me what's going on?" Gayle was on her feet now. She couldn't hear what they were cackling about. "Gayle, we're sorry to call you this late sweetie but Marie insisted" Faye started. Gayle, frustrated now said "Never mind that Faye, what's going on?" Gayle was looking for her sweats and stumbled over something on the floor. "Ouch!" Gayle gasped grabbing her foot. "Calvin and I got into it and I'm over at Marie's. Do you think you could come over?" Faye tried to sugar coat it a little so that Gayle wouldn't worry. Marie grabbed the phone again. "He tried to kill her Gayle. Come over so that we can handle this

74

please" Marie said as a fatter-of-fact. Gayle was dressed and grabbing her purse off of the dresser. "I'm on my way!" she yelled before hanging up. She shook Erik and told him that Marie and Gayle needed her. He grunted something incoherent and she flew down the stairs. She jotted a sloppy note on the notepad of the fridge. Even though she and Erik were at odds, she didn't want him to think she'd left him in the middle of the night.

By the time Gayle got there, everyone was gathered in the living room including Michelle and Anthony. Faye was sitting on the chaise with her feet tucked looking like a little girl. "Did you guys start without me?" Gayle said making her rounds kissing cheeks. Michelle made room on the sofa. "No, Anthony and I just got here" Michelle said. We all looked to Faye to explain what was going on. Michelle was especially worried since Gayle had informed her of the talk that she'd had with Faye at Michael's birthday party. While Faye filled them in, Anthony got everyone cold drinks. He knew Faye's history with men but she didn't deserve this. Faye was like a sister to him. He and Michelle had always sort of protected her ever since he'd known her.

Faye looked around the room at all of her friends and said a silent prayer of thanks for them. "I just don't know what to do" she said. "I feel so helpless. I really thought that Calvin and I had the makings of a good relationship." Michelle was the first to speak up. "Faye now is not the time to criticize you or place blame. We just want you to be alright. Calvin is just a wimp bastard that gets off on controlling his women." Michelle was so pissed. Faye had always fallen in love overnight and then ended up hurt in the end. Everyone gave their two cents worth and the mood seemed to lighten a bit. Anthony went over to the chaise and gave Faye a brotherly hug. "Come on Faye. I'll take you back to your place so that you can grab some of your things. You can stay with us or Marie until you make a decision about when you'll feel comfortable going home." Anthony placed his hand under her chin and looked her in the eye. "You always dive head first Faye. Once you realize that you don't have to save every man you meet, you'll be just fine." He got up and grabbed her hand to help her to her feet. "Come on Lil' Sis, let's go get your things so that you can settle in."

Chapter 27
Love Without A Limit

Anthony and Faye arrived at her house at around four in the morning. Michelle, Gayle and Marie promised to stay up until they returned. They all made Faye promise to call the police to file a report and to get a restraining order. At Faye's house, Anthony entered first to make sure the coast was clear. Faye waited on the porch until he came out and told her it was OK to come in. Faye felt strange in her own home. She'd worked too hard to have something to call her own and now this. She definitely wouldn't let a man make her feel this way again. She grabbed a duffle bag out of the bedroom closet and started throwing in necessities for the next few days. When they got back to Marie's, they were going to go file the restraining order and then maybe she'd feel safer returning home.

Back at Marie's house, Michelle Googled Calvin on the computer. As a financial advisor to the top law and accounting firms in the city, Michelle had connections with agencies that conduct background checks. When Faye initially told her about Calvin's behavior, she had one of the clerks do a background check on him. She never followed through after Faye told her that Calvin was a big shot partner and that she was planning on meeting his family. She assumed that the relationship was a good one until Gayle and Faye had their heart to heart at Michael's party. By then Carol, the clerk at RSC Investigations, was on vacation. Well, she had two hours before their offices opened and she'd put in a call to Carol to see what she'd dug up.

Anthony waited in the living room while Faye got her things together. He dosed off in the recliner when he thought he heard something outside. He got up and went to the living room window and noticed a black Acura in front of Faye's house. The windows were tinted so he couldn't see if someone was inside. Thinking he was probably being overly cautious he went to the kitchen to get something to snack on when he heard what sounded like Faye's muffled yells coming from upstairs. Anthony took the stairs two at a time and looked down the hallway to Faye's bedroom. "Faye, you about ready to go" he asked slowly making his way down the hall. He could hear a man's voice mumbling something. Anthony looked around for something to protect himself and decided on a African statue of a mother and child on the table in the hallway.

Anthony got to the bedroom and used his foot to push open the door. Calvin had Faye by the neck pinned to the wall. Calvin looked in Anthony's direction and yelled "Oh, so is this who you leaving me for Faye, huh?" he said emphasizing his words by squeezing her neck harder and pointing a knife to her face. "How 'bout if I slice your face up so that even *he* won't want to look at your sorry ass." Calvin looked from Faye to Anthony with hatred in his eyes. Anthony tried to think of something to divert Calvin's attention. "Come on man. Faye and I are family. Why don't you let her go and we can talk about this outside, man to man." Anthony moved closer into the room. He made eye contact with Faye and noticed that she had urine coming down her legs. "It's alright Faye." Anthony tried to console her. "Calvin and I are going to take this outside. Just stay calm OK?" Anthony tried to move a little closer. Calvin looked amused. "Oh, so you runnin' things now big man? This here is my woman." Still holding Faye by the neck, Calvin faced Anthony. "She's not going anywhere." He turned back to Faye. "You wanna jump outta cars, huh? I told you to stop disrespecting me Faye." He pointed the knife at her again. "All you had to do was listen. See what happens when you're hard headed?" He finally let her go and she dropped to the floor gasping for air.

Calvin turned to Anthony using the knife to make his point. "See big man, all of this could've been avoided" he sneered. "You know how women can be. They need a stern hand from time to time." Calvin looked over at Faye to make sure she was listening. Anthony took this opportunity and grabbed for the knife. Calvin turned and tried to swing on him. Anthony took a stance and countered with a right to Calvin's chin. Calvin stumbled a bit but came back with a left to the gut followed by an elbow to Anthony's right eye. Anthony had boxed in college but he had to admit, Calvin was a good opponent. Faye looked on in fear. She tried to move around them to get to the telephone that was on the bedside table. She was able to get to it and dialed 911. Just as the operator came on the line, she heard Anthony scream out, "Faye run!" She turned to see Calvin standing over him with the knife dripping with blood. Anthony was wreathing in agony. "911 What is your emergency?" Faye tried to speak but nothing would come out. The operator asked again and Faye could feel herself weakening. She felt like her throat was closing up and she tried to reach out to Anthony but hit the floor and everything went black.

Chapter 28
To Err is Human...

Michelle had just gotten off of the phone with her office telling her assistant that she'd work from home today. She'd already called Anthony's secretary to tell her he'd be out as well. Then she followed up with a call to the kids instructing Alyssa to get the boys up, fed and on the school bus. Alyssa told her mom that she had heard her parents talking in the middle of the night. She overheard something about her auntie Faye being in trouble. She tried to question her mom to see what had happened but Michelle told her that everything was fine and that they'd speak later. Michelle was pre-occupied with thinking what could be taking Anthony and Faye so long to return. Anthony had left his cell phone at home and Faye hadn't answered her house phone.

Michelle looked over at Gayle stretched out on the sofa. Marie was in the kitchen cooking breakfast. She could smell the aroma of bacon and her stomach started to rumble. Just as she picked up the phone to try Faye once more she heard a hard knock on the door. Marie came out of the kitchen wiping her hands with a dish towel. Faye and Anthony would've just walked in. They looked at each other as Michelle joined Marie at the door. Marie looked through the peep hole and whispered, "it's the police." Michelle started to feel sick. She immediately knew that something was very wrong. She nervously wrung her hands as Marie opened the door.

There were two officers, and they looked very young. "Good morning ma'am. Sorry to disturb you but are you Marie Johnson?" he asked hesitantly. "Yes I am. Is there something that I can help you with officer?" She said and reached out to hold Michelle's hand. "My name is Officer Lorenzo Parker. Do you have a friend by the name of Faye Nichols?" he tried to sound as pleasant as possible. He absolutely hated this part of the job. His partner never wanted to do it. They sat in the squad car for ten minutes arguing over who would do the talking. "Yes I do. Is there something wrong? Is she OK" Marie asked desperately. "Well, she…uh, she called the police right before six this morning. The operator couldn't get a response on the other end and it's protocol that a squad car is sent out. Can we come in for a moment please" he didn't want to do this on the front step. He'd rather they be sitting. "Please, just tell us what's wrong officer. My husband is with her." Michelle yelled, her entire body shaking. By this time Gayle was sitting up trying to figure out who was yelling. She saw the officers at the door and jumped to her feet to join Marie and Michelle at the door. He stepped up so that he was a little closer to the three women. Gayle looked to Michelle to get an explanation as to what was going on. "Well Miss, it appears that your husband got into an altercation with Ms. Nichols boyfriend and….." he hated this. "Has Anthony been arrested?" Michelle said stepping face to face with the officer. His partner moved a little in case the woman got hysterical. Gayle quickly grabbed their purses from the foyer table and slid on her shoes. This didn't sound good. "Uh, no not at all ma'am. Your husband has been taken to Howard University Hospital." He looked to his note pad to get the details correct. "The assailant, a Calvin Stevens, had a hunting knife and your husband tried to defend Ms. Nichols. The fight resulted in your husband sustaining an injury." Michelle couldn't have heard him correctly. Anthony was only supposed to go with Faye to get some things and then come back over to Marie's. He had to be mistaken.

Gayle grabbed Michelle who was on her way out of the door. "Wait a minute Chelle." She said taking her hand again. "Officer, you have to tell us. Is Anthony….is he going to be alright?" Gayle had to know before they left for the hospital. "Well, he was in and out of consciousness en route to the hospital but the injury is pretty serious. We should get to the hospital." Michelle felt like her legs were made of Jell-O. She couldn't will them to move until Gayle pulled her by the arm. They drove Marie's BMW while the officer's rode in front, leading with the siren's blaring. Michelle couldn't fathom life without Anthony. He had to be alright…he had to be. She felt as if her breath would leave her body if the hospital told her otherwise. Almost as if she were reading her thoughts, Marie said, "Anthony is going to be just fine, Chelle. He is a strong and healthy man. Let's just get to him" she said taking her eyes off the road to look over at Michelle. "I need you to say to me that he's going to be just fine. Come on…say it." Marie said. Michelle looked ashen. Gayle reached from the back seat to rub Michelle's shoulders. Michelle couldn't figure out how to act. What will she tell the kids? How could things have gone so wrong? "Marie, I love him so much. I can't picture my life….." her words seemed to get caught in her throat. "He has to be fine. I'm claiming it. He just has to come home to me." Michelle looked out the window oblivious to the world passing before her eyes.

Chapter 29
God's Grace is Sufficient

Gayle was the first to enter the emergency room. Marie was closely behind her helping a shaken Michelle. Gayle saw Faye sitting in the waiting room looking as if she was totally unaware of her surroundings. Her blouse was covered with blood. Gayle made her way to Faye while Michelle and Marie went to the desk to inquire about Anthony. The police officers stood off to the side of the entrance waiting for an opportunity to ask more questions. Michelle who usually commanded control of any situation clearly could not get it together. She tried to address the woman behind the admittance counter. "My husband is here. I mean, he was brought in by ambulance. Can you tell me where he is? I need to get to him." She let go of Marie's hand and frantically searched her purse for her wallet. The woman had an obvious attitude and was ready to go home. Her boyfriend hadn't called all day and she couldn't wait to get home and tear into him. She didn't even bother to look up from the computer screen. "Does he have a name ma'am?" Michelle wasn't even aware that the woman had said anything. The hospital seemed to have this smell of sickness and death. Tears slowly started to creep down her face once more.

Marie stepped up to the counter and bent over it to get the woman's attention. "I'm sure you can see that my friend is very upset. You see, her husband could be lying on a cot somewhere dying while you are giving up attitude. Can you kindly help us before I reach over this counter and slap some sense into your young ass?" *Denise*, according to her name tag looked up and saw Marie's face. She quickly regrouped and said in a strained polite voice. "Can I have his name please ma'am?" Marie straightened her stance and took Michelle's purse from her hands. Grateful that Marie had taken control, Michelle gladly handed over the purse. She looked around the room filled with people. Lord, please don't let this be happening. *Did I tell Anthony that I loved him this morning?* "His name is Anthony Moore. He was brought in with a stab wound" Marie said. She was able to fish out Michelle's wallet and found the insurance card that was on the opposite side of a picture of the kids. She'd have to get them from school. Michelle was in no position to face them right now. "Here is his insurance information. Can you hurry please?" Marie said and pulled Michelle a little closer and rubbed her back. The woman disappeared through the double doors leading to the back. She returned with what looked like a nurse. She was a large woman with big hair that took her time getting to them.

"Mrs. Moore?" the nurse said. "Come with me. I'll take you to the attending doctor." She supported Michelle and gave her a reassuring smile. "Don't worry. I'm sure your husband will be just fine." Marie started behind them. "Can I come back with her? I don't want her to be alone." The nurse seemed to be a compassionate woman. She'd probably been doing this for a very long time. "I'm sorry ma'am. No one other than immediate family can go back now. No worries now. I promise to take good care of her." Michelle mustered up what she hoped looked like a smile and told Marie not to worry. She promised to give them word as soon as she spoke to the doctor. And with that Michelle and the nurse disappeared through the double doors. Michelle looked to be almost depending totally on the nurse to support her weight. Marie turned to see where Gayle and Faye were. She spotted them in a corner, Gayle now crying along with Faye. This was going to be a long day.

After what seemed like hours, Michelle appeared in the waiting room. She looked heavy with grief. They all got up from their seats and hurried to her. Faye seemed uncertain and stood closer to Gayle. She knew that this was all her fault. Michelle was closer to her than her own family. If she lost Anthony or Michelle she'd be better off dead. "What did they say, Chelle? How's Anthony?" Gayle asked. They searched her face for a clue. Michelle sat in a chair close by and they gathered around her. The other people in the waiting room seemed to be waiting for an answer too. "The doctor says that Anthony went in to shock by the time he arrived. There's a possibility that one of his lungs may have collapsed. He also said that the knife apparently cut through his small intestine causing fecal matter to leak into his stomach." Michelle felt drained of all of her energy. She closed her eyes, massaging her head to try to relieve some of the pressure.

Marie stooped in front of Michelle and grabbed both her hands. "He'll be fine though right Chelle? I mean those are things that they can correct, right?" Marie prayed that Anthony would pull through this. He was like a brother to all of them. He was always there when any of them needed him. Now he needed them and this is where they'd be until he came through this.
Gayle sat on one side and Faye on the other. They all waited for Michelle's response. "I don't know Marie. He's in a coma now. He lost a lot of blood because the knife was pulled out when he was stabbed. The doctor said they repaired his small intestine and that I'd have to wait 72 hours to see if his lung will return to normal. As for the coma, it's up to God and Anthony's body how long he'll be comatose." Michelle rocked forward and let out a loud wail at the thought of Anthony not coming out of this. She finally cried harder than she'd ever cried in her life. They all hugged and comforted Michelle. Faye knew in her heart that things would never be the same.

Chapter 30
Friend or Foe

The holidays were right around the corner. Anthony had been in a coma for almost a week now. Alyssa and the boys were doing a fine job of trying to keep themselves together. When she told them about the *accident,* AJ had taken it very hard. He and his dad were very close. She hoped she'd been successful in putting on a brave front for them. She told them that their daddy would be just fine. He just needed some time to rest so that he could get better. Alyssa, of course, knew better. She waited for the boys to go downstairs before she started with her questions. She wanted to know why wasn't he conscious yet, and why did auntie Faye's boyfriend do this to him, and when could she go to see her daddy. Michelle tried to be as truthful as she possibly could. She told her about the incident at Faye's. She told her that her dad was in a coma and that he was a fighter so she was sure he'd come through fine. Alyssa was unrelenting. She told her mom that she heard her crying at night. She was not a child and wanted to know the truth. Michelle told her that there was a possibility that her dad may not come through. She told her that the knife wound was very damaging and now it was a waiting game. Alyssa asked if she could go and see him and Michelle agreed. She was impressed by Alyssa's courage. She was such a beautiful girl. Since Anthony was still in the ICU, the boys wouldn't be allowed. Faye had volunteered to sit with them but Michelle wasn't quite ready to face her.

The police caught Calvin three days after the stabbing at a relative of his estranged *wife.* The police later told Michelle that his wife left him after he came to her job to confront her about her supposedly cheating on him with one of her co-workers. When she refused to go outside and talk to him, he proceeded to beat her unmercifully. It took two of his wife's co-workers and the buildings security officer to pull him off of her. She spent two weeks in the hospital with two broken ribs, a concussion, a broken pelvis and a broken eye socket. Not to mention the countless older scars from previous run-ins with Calvin. Apparently, there was a history of abuse and the police had been called to their home on many occasions. Carol, the background investigation clerk, had also over-nighted the file that had his arrest history. Calvin had spent the better part of his young adult life in jail for assault, petty theft and distribution.

Michelle tried to keep a sense of normalcy in her home. She continued to busy herself by cooking and cleaning and taking the kids to their perspective activities. She'd worked from home and distributed some of her more pending projects to two of her employees. Fred, Anthony's operational manager had always done well running things in Anthony's absence. He'd been a trusted friend for over ten years. Michelle knew that the trucks would be serviced and the staff would be supervised. Anthony had regular clients, so she could always oversee the workload occasionally to make sure all was well. Fred gave her a weekly report and sent one of the guys over to shovel snow and put down salt in front of the house for her. Gayle and Marie called and came over almost daily to check on her. Faye had called also but Michelle never picked up. Faye left message after message offering to keep the kids or to come over just to sit with her. Faye finally called Gayle in desperation. Gayle told her to give Michelle some time. She was under a lot of stress and probably just didn't feel like talking right now.

Faye hadn't slept well or eaten in days. She went to the hospital to sit with Anthony when she knew Michelle had left to pick up the kids. The doctors said that he was stabilized but he was still in a coma. She whispered how sorry she was and begged him to please get better. Anthony had never judged her. Whenever a relationship went south or when her prior so called boyfriend stole all of her furniture, he never said a word. He went out and got her a television and had one of the guys at the shop load up the couch that was in their basement and brought it over until she could get more furniture. He and Michelle had always been there.

Faye hadn't spoken to her parents in over three years. Her mom had always told her that she wouldn't amount to anything. Her mother never wanted children and her father was never at home. He would stay at work just so he wouldn't have to come home and hear his wife's constant berating. Faye was so grateful when she was accepted to North Carolina A&T. She'd stay on campus during the holidays. During the summer, she'd take extra classes so that people didn't wonder why she didn't go home. That's where she met Michelle. She was on her way to the deli/convenience store where everyone went for lunch. There was a stray cat out front. When Faye was younger she fed every stray in the neighborhood. She would build makeshift shelters for them in the field behind their house. She stooped to rub the kitty when she heard a voice behind her saying that she shouldn't rub him because he could be carrying all kinds of diseases. When Faye stood and turned towards the lady standing behind her, she saw Michelle in an olive green pea coat with her long hair piled on top of her head and reading glasses pushed up on her forehead. At first Faye thought that maybe she was one of the professors but thought she was very young to be a professor. Michelle introduced herself and offered Faye some antibacterial hand sanitizer. Michelle asked her if she'd eaten and invited her to sit with her and her friends for lunch. Faye couldn't remember a time since then when her girls weren't around.

Michelle and Marie were in their sophomore year and Faye and Gayle were in their freshman year when they all became friends. Gayle and Michelle's parents were old friends so it was Michelle's job to show Gayle the ropes of college life. Marie and Michelle were assigned a dorm room together and hit it off. Michelle had always been the grounded one. Gayle was the one that rallied for every cause she could think of. Marie was the unapproachable one. Guys were always intimidated by her brash attitude and stand-off approach. Faye was the gullible one that took everyone at their word. They all kind of relied on each other and since then, they'd been a part of each other's lives.

Chapter 31
Test of Your Faith

After her usual routine, Michelle got to the hospital a little after nine. She'd gotten to know the nurses that were attending to Anthony and she waived at Pauline as she entered his room. Pauline would be here until five and then Constance would be here throughout the evening. She was lucky the nurses took very good care of him. Yesterday she walked in on Pauline reading a Dr. Seuss book to Anthony. Michelle stood at the door smiling until Pauline noticed her. She said she was hoping Anthony would wake up and tell her enough of the kiddy stuff already. Anthony was moving his head and his hands occasionally moved from time to time but that was about it. Pauline made her exit and pulled the door shut behind her.

Michelle squeezed beside Anthony on the hospital bed so that she'd be close to his ear. She always talked to him as if he was fully aware of what she was saying. She'd give him reports about the business, the kids, what was the latest trash on the boob tube. He looked like he was sleeping peacefully. She loved to watch him sleep. Anthony had the ability to fall asleep anywhere. He always told her that it was because he worked so hard. She thought back to what seemed like ages ago. "I remember the first time I saw you" she said. You had on old ripped jeans and boots with a NHRA t-shirt and those broad shoulders were bulging. Marie and I were in a carry-out picking up our food when you walked in with a friend of yours. I remember shoving Marie and looking in your direction so that she could see how good you looked. You brushed by me to get in line and I could smell your cologne. Umph…you smelled so good." Michelle laid her head on Anthony's chest as she thought back to that day. "You said hello to us, but you were looking directly at me. Even though we had already ordered, I had Marie get another order of fries just so I could look at you a little longer. When we left, you guys were still inside. As soon as we got outside, I told Marie that you were so fine." Michelle sighed and tucked the covers in around Anthony. "Ya know, Marie tried to make me go back in to get your phone number, but I was not the type to approach guys. They always approached me." Michelle laughed a little. Back then, she had the guys eating out of her hands. She was always called a "good girl", because she went to church, didn't hang out on the corner and always demanded respect from the guys. Her dad also made it very clear that he wouldn't tolerate any foolishness. As a result, the guys in the neighborhood looked out for her.

"I didn't think anything of it when Marie said that she'd left her drink on the counter. I told her I'd meet her back at the house. Since we lived only a block from the carry-out, by the time I reached my porch she wasn't far behind. She was grinning from ear to ear and I had to practically hit her to get her to tell me what she'd done. When she told me that she'd given you my number I could've died. I was so embarrassed. She was like "Oooh Michelle, his name is Anthony and he is feeling you girl. He said he's definitely going to call you." I told her about herself and then went in the house and didn't come back out that evening." She cuddled a little more closer to Anthony. She'd missed him laying in bed beside her. They'd never spent a night apart with the exception of Michelle's stay in the hospital giving birth to the kids. Even then, Anthony would camp out in a chair or squeeze into bed with her at the hospital.

"When you first called me, I pretended not to remember who you were. I never told you that." She kissed him on the cheek. "I actually waited for you to call me. Even though you were a little older than me, there was something about you. You had this presence….it's hard to explain. I loved the way you spoke to me, like I was the only person that existed. I remember thinking that the girls must just throw themselves at you. I pretended to play tough and put you off but I looked forward to the long talks we'd have. You seemed to know just what to say. I guess that was your Mack daddy routine in full effect, huh" she smiled. *Come on baby. Give me something. Smile at me. Squeeze my hand.* The threat of tears came and she fought them off. The doctors told her that he shouldn't be stressed at all. She wanted him to know that she was there. She wanted him to feel her heart and open his eyes and take her into his arms. She ached for it. She continued to tell him how he'd won her over. She put her head on his chest and rubbed the back of his hand. His left hand looked odd without his wedding band. She didn't realize she drifted off to sleep until Pauline came in and tried quietly to check his fluids. Michelle opened her eyes and stretched a little. Pauline said that she tried not to wake her. She knew how exhausted she must be.

Michelle was glad Pauline came in. It was almost time for her to leave to pick up the kids. Alyssa had practice tonight and stressed that she couldn't be late. On Saturday Michelle would bring the kids for a visit. Pauline said she would let them peek in for just a second. The kids were relentless and she tried to put it off for as long as possible. She didn't want the kids to see their dad like this. He was always so strong and had such a rapport with them. She didn't want them to be afraid when they saw him. Especially Michael. His dad represented the world to him. There was nothing his dad couldn't fix or do. His daddy even tied his shoes better than mommy. Alyssa was also different somehow. She was starting to get very secretive and that worried Michelle. She guessed it was the whole pre-teen thing. She wished Anthony had a chance to have a man to man with Terrell. She tried to trust Alyssa but it was hard for her to leave her at dance practice and not sit in the audience. There seemed to be so much going on with work and the kids and Anthony these days.

Michelle was worried she'd miss a sign or some indication that Alyssa was in trouble. If only Anthony were here, he'd make things right. Michelle kissed him again and whispered she loved him in his ear. She squeezed his hand and let her lips linger on his for a moment. She thought she felt movement in his hand. It was just a slight squeeze. It happened so quick that she almost missed it. She couldn't have been imagining it. She looked over at Pauline who was writing something in his chart. "He squeezed my hand a little Pauline. He did." Pauline came over and used the pen light to check his eyes. She used her pen to swipe the bottom of his feet for an indication that he'd felt something. Her face showed her disappointment. She told Michelle that she didn't see any change. "Sometimes nerves will cause a jump or the eyelids to flutter. While

90

it's a good sign, these things are normal in coma patients." Michelle pulled Pauline over towards the door and whispered to her, "I felt it Pauline. I've talked to him every day for almost three weeks. I always hold his hand and watch his eyes. I've watched him breathe. I watch everything hoping that he would react to my voice. This is the first time he's squeezed my hand. I'm telling you, this was different." Michelle was hanging on to every hope. Pauline said that after her rounds, she come in and sit with him for a while. She promised to call if something changed. Pauline had been a nurse for ten years and she'd seen a lot. She'd never tell Michelle that a simple hand movement didn't mean much. He could come out of this tomorrow or he could stay comatose for another month. You could never tell.

Chapter 32
Who said Forgiveness was Divine

Michelle and the boys sat at the kitchen table. Thanksgiving was approaching fast and she wasn't in a very thankful mood these days. While the boys ate their snack, Michelle got paper and pencils out of the island drawer. "It's that time boys. I make my call to Santa next week and I need to know what you naughty boys want for Christmas. AJ used his sleeve to wipe off his milk mustache. He waited for his mom to sit back down and leaned over to whisper in her ear. "Mom, don't you think I'm getting a little too old for this? I mean, I know that daddy is Santa." Michelle slid Michael's cookies a little closer so he wouldn't make a mess. She gave AJ a goofy look and shushed him. Michelle knew that AJ didn't believe anymore. "Start writing AJ." She winked at him. Michael, who was sitting on the opposite side of her was busy concentrating on writing his letters to care about what AJ was saying. He was getting a little frustrated because he couldn't get the "C" in truck quite right. Michelle reached over and helped him hold his pencil properly. "Remember I told you, it's just like an "O" but it's open on this side." She said tracing the letter with her finger.

Satisfied with his list, he hopped down out of his chair to show his list to AJ. AJ looked it over and reminded him that he the wanted the Spiderman web shooter that he saw on the commercial. AJ wrote it in for him. Michael looked at the list once more and said, "I'm all done mommy!" He proudly handed over the paper with big shaky letters. "Do you think I could talk to Santa when you call?" Michael said. AJ laughed as he got up to put his saucer and glass in the sink. He came over and hugged Michelle around her neck as he stood behind her chair. "Yeah mom, can I talk to Santa too?" AJ said giggling. He couldn't wait to see how his mom would answer. Michelle reached around and pinched AJ on the butt. She turned to

Michael and cupped his face in her hands. "Santa only talks to
adults on the phone, baby. See, sometimes kids will fib about if
they've been naughty or nice. So Santa only talks to kids when he
comes out to the malls and to school. This way you can sit on his
lap to tell him what you'd like. Then later he talks to the parents to
get a report on how good the children really are." AJ tickled
Michael and he squealed. "You're outta luck then buddy. Santa's
gonna put coal under the tree for you." AJ teased him. "I've been a
good boy, right mommy?" Michael play boxed AJ. Michelle got up
and went to the sink to wash the few dishes in the sink. "Yes, you
have baby. AJ's the one that will have a "coal" Christmas."
Michelle made a goofy face at AJ. "Get it AJ? A "Coal"
Christmas!" Michelle laughed at her feeble attempt at making a
joke. AJ playfully jabbed Michael in the side. "Very funny
mom…so funny I forgot to laugh." Michelle took the towel and
swatted them both on the bottom. She told Michael to go upstairs to
get his shoes.

Today was the day that they were going to see Anthony in the
hospital. Alyssa was upstairs doing her hair. AJ hung back and
waited until he heard Michael reach the top of the stairs. He leaned
against the counter and looked over to his mom. "Mom, dad will be
here for Christmas won't he? I mean I just want to know for
Michael. Who'll put on the goofy Santa hat and eat the cookies and
milk if dad isn't here?" Michelle had to turn away for a moment.
He'd caught her off guard. AJ tried to be such a big boy, but she
knew he was hurting inside. She reached over and pulled him close
to her. Since he proclaimed that he was not a little boy anymore,
their hugs and kisses were limited. She didn't want to embarrass
him. She still had a few more years to baby Michael. "I sure hope
so son. I know you miss him AJ and that's OK." She could see
tears forming in his eyes and she held him a little tighter. "Your dad
is in good health. It's up to his body to heal so that his brain will
release him from this deep sleep. It's also important that we
continue to pray and ask God to bring him through this." She
wondered if she believed what she was saying. She'd found herself
being almost angry with God for allowing this to happen. "This
family has been through some things AJ. I'm positive that this too
shall pass." She lifted his chin and rubbed noses with him. "You've

93

grown so much. You are becoming more and more like your daddy every day. I am very proud of how you're taking care of Michael. Thanks baby." She hugged him tight. He hung on to her and said a silent prayer that his dad would come home soon. He wasn't quite ready to be the man of the house just yet.

Michelle tidied up a bit more while the kids were upstairs getting ready. She heard the doorbell ring as she took out chicken breasts for dinner. She got to the door and looked through the peephole. Michelle rung her hands and paced for a moment thinking if she should open the door. Faye waited on the other side. She knew they were home because she saw Michelle's truck in the driveway. She never parked in the garage. Faye knocked this time. After another minute, she raised her fist to knock again when Michelle slowly opened the door.

Faye smiled nervously unconsciously adjusted her coat to avoid eye contact. "Hey Chelle. I hadn't heard from you or the troop in a while so......I just wanted to drop in on ya." Faye said trying to look pass her to see if she could get a glimpse of one of the kids. Michelle stood directly in front of the door blocking her view. "Hello Faye." She said a little too formally. "You should've called first. We're on our way to the hospital." Faye walked a little closer to Michelle. "I have called you Michelle. Why haven't you called me back? I've been trying to get a hold of you to see how you were doing." Faye finally looked her in the eye and almost cried. Michelle looked so tired and so, so sad. Michelle's anger came from nowhere. Her grip tightened on the door knob. "My husband is in the hospital Faye." Michelle had to almost whisper so that the children wouldn't hear. "How do you think I'm doing? My children are afraid that their dad won't ever come home. So you tell me, how do you think I should feel?" Michelle looked at Faye in both anger and love. She missed her too but she needed someone to take the fall for all of this mess.

Faye let the tears fall. She didn't blame Michelle for hating her. She hated herself for what had happened. "Michelle, please don't do this. Don't shut me out. I need you to...." Before Michelle knew what she'd done she slapped Faye across her face. "Don't you dare tell me what you need Faye." Michelle immediately regretted what she'd done. Faye put her hand to her face and cried. "Chelle I didn't mean for any of this to happen. You know that I would never put Anthony in any danger." Michelle could tell that Faye was just as exhausted and devastated as she was. She knew in her heart that Faye was not the blame for what had happened. The man responsible was behind bars and would hopefully stay there. Faye continued to cry in her hands. Michelle stepped out on the porch and grabbed her by the shoulders. They looked at each other for a long time. Finally, Michelle pulled her close and they cried together. They cried for each other. They cried for Anthony. They cried for a friendship that was almost lost.

Chapter 33
Fervent and Unmovable

Michelle, Faye and the kids finally made it to the hospital. Upon entering Anthony's room, Michelle noticed that her parents, Gayle and Marie were already there. Michelle's mom was cleaning Anthony's face. Her dad looked up from his chair beside the bed. Gayle and Marie were standing at the foot of the bed. Michael let go of Michelle's hand and ran over to his grandmother. "Granny, you didn't tell me you were coming." Michelle's mom scooped Michael up in her arms and kissed his cheek. He looked at Anthony like nothing had changed. "Hey daddy, why in the world is granny washing your face? You're a big boy, you can wipe your own face." Michael looked from his dad to Michelle. His face asking the question why wasn't his dad answering him. Michelle reached out for AJ's hand. Alyssa was standing closely behind her mom. Michelle smiled at everyone and moved closer to the bed. "Michael, daddy is in a very deep sleep sweetie. He can hear you but he can't answer you." Michelle went over and kissed her parents. Her dad told her that their pastor had just left. He prayed with Anthony and said he would return in a few days. They'd been members of Faith Baptist for a long time and had a good relationship with the pastor and first lady. She'd have to remember to call them later to thank them for coming out.

Marie went over and hugged AJ and then Alyssa. Both Gayle and Marie gave Faye a smile of relief. It was obvious that she and Michelle had resolved any issues they had. "Hey guys, come on in. It's all right." Marie said to the kids. She squeezed Michelle's shoulder as she and the kids made their way back over to the bed. Gayle moved back against the wall to give them room. She held out her hand and Faye gratefully accepted. Alyssa and AJ hugged and kissed their grandparents. They stood near the window on the left

96

side of the bed. Gayle, Faye and Marie excused themselves so that the kids could have some time with their dad. The room had become quite crowded. They took Michelle's parents with them and went to the cafeteria for coffee. Michael, still a little confused grabbed Alyssa's hand. She lifted him up so that he could have a better view.

Alyssa looked at her dad lying in bed. He was such a big man that he took up most of the bed. "Is it OK if I give him a kiss mom?" She looked at Michelle for direction. "He has all of those wires hooked up to him. I don't want to screw anything up" Alyssa said. "Of course you can give him a kiss Lyssie." Michelle walked around to the side of the bed that they were on. "Baby, look who came to see you." she said to Anthony. She stood behind them and gently pushed them closer to the bed. Alyssa started. "Look at you dad. You'd do anything to get some R&R" she laughed nervously. "I miss you so much daddy. Things just aren't the same at home without you. We can't wait for you to get outta here." She looked back at her mom who encouraged her to go on. Michael reached out to touch his dad's face. "Daddy you need to shave. Your face is rough." He looked at AJ who was standing stiffly beside Alyssa. "Touch daddy's face AJ. It feels like he has a brush growing on his face." Michael smiled almost as if he was trying to encourage AJ. AJ moved a little closer and leaned over and rubbed Anthony's face. "Michael's right dad, you have the werewolf look going on." They seemed to be loosening up a little more. Michelle asked Michael over Alyssa's shoulder. Sweetie, would you like to go to the machine and get a snack with me?" Michael scooted out of Alyssa's arms and pulled his mom to hurry. "Let's go mommy. I'm going to get daddy something too. I'll bet he wakes up for Oreo's!" he said. Michelle wanted to give Alyssa and AJ a few moments alone with Anthony. "She rubbed his foot as she walked by the foot of the bed. "I'll be back in a sec baby." She said to him. This boy really wants his snack." She smiled at her older two and took Michael down the hall to the vending machine.

AJ walked around to the opposite side of the bed. This way they were on either side of Anthony. Alyssa leaned in close. "All right old man. It's time to stop faking and open your eyes and talk to me." She held his hand and rubbed his cheek with the other. AJ

97

placed his hand in his dad's other hand. He leaned in to whisper to his dad. "Alyssa's become absolutely unbearable dad. She's driving me and Michael crazy. If you don't come home soon, they're gonna check us in here for delirium." Alyssa made a face at AJ and she smiled. He and Alyssa had an amazingly good relationship. They fought too but they always seemed to get along more than they fought. Anthony's eyes fluttered a little. Alyssa noticed and leaned in closer. "Come on daddy. I know you can hear me. We need you home with us." She felt herself getting emotional. On the way to the hospital, Michelle told them to stay positive. She told them that even though they were sad, they should be strong for their dad. AJ took his turn. "We've been putting in our requests for Thanksgiving dad, and if you don't hurry home Mom will attempt to make the stuffing. You can't let that happen." Both he and Alyssa laughed at that. Everyone agreed that their dad made the best stuffing ever. Both Anthony's parents had passed on, but Anthony always told them that his mom was an awesome cook. She made sure he knew his way around the kitchen.

Anthony could hear them talking and tried to will himself to open his eyes. He was so tired. He felt like his body was made of cement. Michelle and Michael came back with enough snacks for everyone. Michael bound into the room, "Lyssie, they had M&M's in the machine. The ones with the peanuts just like you like em." He gave Alyssa the bag of candy. "Thanks squirt. You do love me huh?" She said tickling him under his chin. Michelle went over to the bed beside AJ. "These kids are getting away with everything while you're here Anthony. They know mom is a pushover and they're all taking advantage of me." She rubbed his head and leaned in and kissed him on the lips. "Eeew!" Michael said. She smiled at them. Lord knows she didn't know what she'd do without them. They gave her a run for her money but she wouldn't trade them for anything.

She turned back to Anthony. "They need you baby. We all do. Come on and open those beautiful brown eyes and make my day." She took his hand in hers and kissed every finger. "This family isn't complete without you. We can't do this by ourselves." Michael pulled the chair up to the side of the bed. He stood on it and reached into his jeans pocket and pulled out a folded piece of construction paper. He took his time unfolding it and smoothed it out on his thigh. "I made this for you daddy." He turned the picture so that it was right in front of Anthony. "See, it's you and me in your work truck. Remember you promised me that I could shift the stick for you while you drove." He slid the picture under Anthony's pillow. "I'm gonna leave this here so you won't forget, OK daddy?" Satisfied with himself, Michael jumped down and moved the chair over to the television. He turned until he found a channel showing cartoons. AJ excused himself and went to the bathroom that was inside the room. Michelle fixed Anthony's covers for the second time and looked around the room. He had flowers all over from the church, their neighbors and the two bouquets that she had sent from her and the kids. She told the kids that they'd be leaving in a few so that their dad could rest.

Anthony tried his best to tell them not to leave. He willed his body to cooperate. This wasn't him at all. He'd never succumb to this. Lord please give me the strength. I've served you without fail. I've sought you in every aspect of my life. I need you Lord. I can't leave my wife and my babies. There is so much unfinished business that I need to take care of. He hadn't talked to Anthony Jr. about girls yet. *He and Alyssa were supposed to go out on a date so that she could see how a real man treats a young lady. Michael still needed practice with throwing the football. Move! Move! He willed his hands. He could feel his fingers tingling like his hands had fallen asleep.* Once AJ came out of the bathroom, Michelle had Alyssa take Michael to the bathroom. She didn't want any emergencies in the car ride home. *Don't leave Chelle. I'm trying. Stay here with me baby.* Every sound in the room seemed to be amplified. He could hear the toilet flushing. He could hear Michelle zip Michael's coat. *What was happening here? He could feel his whole body shivering.* Michelle and the kids kissed him once more and they started to file out. She told him she'd see him tomorrow morning. Pauline was coming in just as they were leaving.

They walked out to the lounge area. Her parents, Faye, Gayle and Marie were watching a re-run of Law and Order. Michael ran over and sat in Faye's lap. "I missed you Auntie Faye. Did you miss me too?" She hugged him tight and kissed his chubby cheek. "You bet I missed you. You still owe me a dinner date and I'm holding you to it!" Faye hoped that one day she'd have a son just like Michael. He never noticed her flaws. She never knew why she was his favorite. Gayle and Marie tried feverishly to win him over but to no avail. Everyone slid into their coats and Michelle's parents said they'd check in with her during the week. Since they were retired, they could sit with Anthony during the day. Eventually, Michelle would have to return to the office. They made their way to the bank of elevators down the hall. Michelle happened to turn towards the window to see if the promise of snow was true when she saw Pauline running.

Not knowing what to think, she took off running in her direction. Pauline was winded when she reached Michelle. By this time the others noticed what was happening and hurried towards them. "Pauline, what is it?! What is it?!" Michelle had to stop herself from shaking her. "Come quick!" Pauline said. "He's waking up!" Everyone started yelling and crying and laughing all at the same time. Other nurses and people in the lounge looked on wondering what happened. Michelle yelled out "Thank you Jesus!" and raised her hands in total submission. She openly cried and hugged Pauline and she motioned for everyone to come on! Pauline regained her composure and told them that only Michelle could go in. Anthony had sustained a tremendous shock and needed to be brought back to reality slowly. Pauline took Michelle's hand and Michelle almost dragged her down the hall. Michelle entered the room and hurried over to the bed. The doctor was there tending to Anthony. Anthony looked like a bear coming out of hibernation. He was a bit shaken up but fully aware of his surroundings. Michelle laid her head on his chest and cried tears of relief. She could feel Anthony's arms envelope her. "I told you Pauline. I told you he'd come back to me." Pauline couldn't help herself. She started crying too.

The doctor kind of felt out of place witnessing this, so he hurried to scribble something in Anthony's chart and told Michelle that he'd speak to her before she left and then took his exit. "Welcome back baby. I missed you so much." Michelle said. Anthony had to clear his throat several times before the words would come out. "I missed you too Chelle. You have no idea. You didn't give up on me did ya baby?" he asked holding her as tight as he could. His arms were very weak. His voice was raspy and he spoke in a whisper. "I heard you Chelle. I could feel your heart breaking every time you had to leave." Michelle looked up at him and kissed him over and over again. "Shhh Anthony, save your energy baby." She looked over to Pauline who had ruined her makeup crying. "Come over and meet him Pauline. Anthony, this is Pauline." She pulled a hesitant Pauline by the arm closer to the bed. "She took such good care of you for the last few weeks. She took care of me too." Michelle smiled at her. Pauline shook Anthony's hand. "You had a lot of people pulling for you Anthony. It's good to finally hear your voice" she said. Anthony smiled at her. "I could see why you two got along so well. Chelle, she's bossy too" he teased. "She'd come and start right in on me. *Are we waking up today Mr. Moore? If you don't wake up, we'll be reading Dr. Seuss again today Mr. Moore"* he laughed and then rubbed his throat. "She's part of the reason I woke up. I couldn't take another *"Sam I Am"* he said smiling. Pauline left to give them some privacy. Michelle leaned over and kissed him long and hard. "I love you man" she said. Anthony took her face in his hands. "I love you more my love." They were silent for a few moments.

Before Michelle could go out to get the kids to bring them in, they were making their way into the room. All three of them ran over to the bed and planted sloppy kisses and hugs on Anthony. Michelle laughed and tears streamed down her face. Pauline made an exception and let everyone else in also. They all laughed and cried some more. After about twenty minutes, Pauline came in and told them that was it, they had to go. Anthony was visibly tired and needed his rest. They said their goodbye's but Anthony had already drifted off into a peaceful sleep. Faye and Marie took the kids home while Michelle stayed around to talk to the doctor and make sure Anthony was settled in. The doctor said that the wound was healing nicely. His lungs were excellent and as soon as they ran a few tests Anthony would be coming home. Thanksgiving was next week, and they could eat turkey sandwiches for all she cared, as long as Anthony was home.

Chapter 34
I Wish It Would Rain

Marie hung up the phone and tried to gather her strength. She'd been talking to Chelle, Gayle and Faye all morning about what she was about to do. She hadn't heard Parnell's voice in over a month and was starting to think he'd totally forgotten about her. He sent her a couple of emails but they were very impersonal, not at all like him. She made up her mind that she would drive to New York and confront him once and for all about their *relationship*. She wanted him to know that it was nothing that he'd done. She was afraid of another failed relationship. She was foolish and guarded, but she was ready now. His website said that he was doing a book signing at Hue-Man bookstore in Harlem at two, and she planned to be there. *Borderline Blues* was still on the best sellers list. He'd told her that he was hard at work on his next book. *Maybe that's why he hadn't called lately.* Who was she kidding, she'd hurt him. She was at fault and it was time she fessed up to it. She packed a lunch and some other necessities in her car. She double checked to make sure she had a copy of the book. She did a final once over in the mirror by the front door and she was off.

Three hours into her ride she switched from the Luther Vandross CD to the radio, and laughed out loud when she heard the song that was playing. *Sunshine, blue skies, please go away. My girl has found another and gone away. With her went my future, my life is filled with gloom. So day after day, I stayed locked up in my room. I know to you, it might sound strange. But I wish it would rain. (How I wish that it would rain). Oh, yeah, yeah, yeah, yeah.* Lately, it seemed like every time she turned on the radio, a song was playing about lost love. She turned up the volume. *'Cause so badly I wanna go outside. (Such a lovely day). But everyone knows that a man ain't suppose to cry, listen. I gotta cry 'cause cryin' eases the pain, oh yeah. People this hurt I feel inside, words can never explain. I just wish it would rain. (Oh, how I wish that it would rain).* The only difference is that the shoe is on the other foot. She'd never felt like this before. She made sure she was in complete control of every relationship she'd been in. Parnell was very different from the other men that she'd dated in the past. He knew exactly what he wanted. She didn't have a problem wanting him to lead. She hoped it wasn't too late.

The bookstore was very crowded. The salespeople had used the number system to allow everyone an opportunity to meet Parnell. He was seated at a table with two women on either side of him. She hoped that they worked for him and that he wasn't dating one. He looked great in a pair of jeans with black boots. His black sport jacket and matching turtle neck lay on him just right. Marie stood in the back of the waiting area. Her number was 72. *Good grief, what number where they on?* She thought to herself. The women came out in their finest to get a look at Mr. Hawkins. She couldn't blame them. He was indeed a sight for sore eyes. She took her seat and waited patiently. She spent hours choosing what she'd wear today. Not wanting to appear too desperate. She had on a black wrap dress that showed off her curves and a hint of cleavage. Her black boots with stiletto hills only added to her already statuesque frame. She had her hair pulled back and it flowed a little past her shoulders. The black full length cashmere coat and Roberto Cavalli shades gave a hint of mystery. She wasn't usually in the habit of being in pursuit, but these were extreme circumstances. She took hints from the two freaks Michelle and Gayle on how to best approach this situation. She hoped it would work.

After successfully staying out of direct eyesight of Parnell for the last hour, she was now fourth in line. She couldn't believe some of the things these women said to him. The one at the table now was asking him if those big strong hands were evidence of the other gifts he had to offer. She wanted to tap her on the shoulder and tell her that she could attest that he did in fact have a great gift, but that she planned to reap those benefits tonight. Parnell never looked up from the book. He simply thanked the woman for being a fan and asked who he should make the book out to. The woman gave her name and as she took the book, she slid him her card. He passed it on to the woman sitting to his right. The woman looked bored and Marie guessed that she was one of his assistants and used to women throwing themselves at Parnell. She took the card from him and put it with a stack of others. She said "next" as if she was anxious to get these proceedings over with.

Marie stepped up to the table. Parnell took a sip of his water and never looked up. He placed the bottled water back on the floor next to him and took the book from her hand. He made small talk and asked how long she'd been a fan. Marie was a little nervous and the women sitting at the table seemed to be gawking at her. "Actually Mr. Hawkins, I've been your biggest fan since you released your first book." Marie's heart was in her throat. Her hands were shaking a bit so she stuffed them into her coat pockets. Parnell immediately recognized her voice and looked up at her. He let his eyes wander down and then back up. He had to admit, she was looking good enough to eat. "Marie. It's so good to see you." He got up to hug her across the table. The two women looked at each other and then at Marie like *who the hell is this.* As she hugged Parnell, she have them both the evil eye. As he released her from his embrace, she stepped back a little off balance. *Get it together Marie. Now is not the time to act like a klutz.*

He sat back in his chair and Marie could hear the women behind her getting impatient. She got herself together and said, "I heard that you'd be signing here today and thought I'd come see my favorite author in action." She smiled sincerely. He smiled back and noticed again how beautiful she was. "Well, should I make the book out to Marie Johnson then?" He said with his pen poised wondering what brought her to New York. She looked him directly in the eye and leaned close to the table. She lost all of her inhibitions. "What if you make it out to Marie, the love I thought I lost." She said. He looked into her eyes and couldn't believe she'd just said that. They seemed to be stuck in time when one of the women sitting next to him whispered that he should keep it moving. He looked a little taken aback and said, "Right, right. Ugh....Marie, do you think you could wait in the seating area for a minute? I'll be finished here in about 20 minutes or so." Relieved, Marie tried to contain her excitement. "Sure Mr. Hawkins. I'll be waiting over by the café. Can I still have my book signed, please?" she said. He looked down like he hadn't realized he still had her book. She waited for him to sign although she couldn't see what he'd written. He closed the book quickly and gave it to her. She took one last look at the two hounds sitting beside him and walked purposefully over to the café.

As soon as she got a vanilla chamomile tea from the café, she sat at a table and fished out her cell phone. As soon as Gayle answered she immediately started telling Gayle about what had happened. Gayle didn't seem as enthused as she'd hoped. "Well what the hell flew up your butt?" Marie said. Gayle paused on the other end. "Nothing girl, I told you that we had the full proof plan. Parnell loves you Marie. We all could see it in the way that he looked at you. You were the only one who had doubts." Gayle said casually. "Listen, you can fill me in on all the details when you get home. I'm taking care of something right now." Gayle didn't want to steal her joy. She and Erik were in the midst of a serious conversation. Marie was so excited, she was oblivious to the sadness in Gayle's voice. "OK Gayle. Well, I should be home late tonight. I just need to explain things to Parnell." Marie said opening the cover of the book. He wrote, *To Marie, Are You Sure You're Ready for Me? Parnell.* Marie's smile faded a little. This wasn't going to be as easy as she'd thought. She spotted him finishing up and wanted to hurry off of the phone. Gayle wanted to hang up also. "Well call me when you get home then. Good luck and try not to act too desperate." Gayle said. Marie smiled and called her a wench and hung up the phone. She had enough time to adjust her stockings that had rolled down her stomach before Parnell reached the table.

Once Parnell reached the table, he stood there for a moment with a slight grin on his face. She was a little uncomfortable and unsure of what to say. He finally took his seat. "You know you made a lot of ladies upset." He took her hands from across the table. "I know you didn't come all the way to New York just to get your booked signed Marie." He rubbed the back of her hands with his thumbs. "Why don't you tell me the real reason you're here." He always looked her directly in the eye. She squirmed in her seat a little. She focused on the cup that she had in front of her. "Parnell, these last few weeks have given me an opportunity to do a lot of thinking." She peeked up at him and he held her gaze. She looked down at his hands holding hers. Her stomach felt upset and she thought she was going to lose it right on the table. He sat silently waiting for her to continue. He didn't seem to enjoy seeing her gravel, but he made no attempt to stop her either.

"The thing is…I've tried to keep my distance when it came to men. I always said when and where. It was usually me that determined when the relationship would end." Marie closed her eyes for moment. "I'm not even sure if I've ever really been in love. My relationships just seemed to exist." She couldn't really think with him holding her hands so she slowly pulled away from his grasp and put her hands in her lap. "What I'm trying to say is that I'm sorry for not allowing you fully into my heart. I didn't realize that I'd fallen in love with you until you dropped me off that night. Even then, I didn't have the courage to tell you." Parnell pulled his chair around to her side of the small table. He put his hand on her leg and gently squeezed. "I've missed you Marie. For a long time I put off relationships because I wanted to focus on my writing. I wanted to be able to fully commit instead of having a fling in whatever city I happened to be in." She finally had the courage to look at him. He felt so right. *Please God have favor on me. I promise to love him with everything I've got if you'll give me one more chance.* Parnell went on, "After I left you that night, it took every bit of will power that I could muster not to come back to you. I want you to know that I won't go through that again, Marie." She could feel herself stiffen. What was he saying? "You have to want me Marie. You have to be sure that this is what you want. I'm willing to love you through this uncertainty that you have about relationships, but I won't be subject to you purposely hurting me because you're afraid to love me." He touched her face and she almost melted. She felt herself lean into him. "It's nothing wrong with being a little vulnerable Marie. I told you what I wanted. I've put all of the dating do's and don'ts on the back burner. I've always told you that you are what I want. Can you honestly say the same thing?" He folded his arms on the table and hoped he made himself clear.

Marie mustered her courage and rested her hand on one of his. "I will….I mean, I do want you Parnell. I promise to try to stop being so guarded all of the time. It's how I've survived for so long. I didn't even realize I was being so limited until you came along." She leaned on his shoulder and closed her eyes. "How do we do this? You live here and I live in Maryland." She wanted to be near him as much as possible. Parnell leaned in closer to her. "You forget I write for a living. I can do that anywhere. I can split my time between here and DC. This will give you an opportunity to let your employees work and you can come and spend some weekends in the big city with me." They looked at each other and finally he kissed her. Marie didn't care who watched. She kissed Parnell with urgency like he'd disappear if she let go of him. She realized that she really did love him more than she thought.

Chapter 35
Layered Love

This year Gayle and Erik were supposed to host the Thanksgiving dinner at their house but since Anthony was still healing, they all agreed to have it at Michelle's. Dinner was scheduled for three. They always made plans for early in the day so that they'd have time to chat and play games before sitting down to dinner. Michelle fussed over Anthony making sure he was comfortable in the family room. He tried to give up some opposition but Michelle won him over. She did allow him to sit at the table earlier to help AJ cut up onions, celery, peppers and to season the Turkey. After that she carted him to the family room and his recliner making him promise not to move and get in her way. She and Alyssa had on their aprons and was back and forth doing this and that in the kitchen. They'd cleaned the house the evening before and they rose early this morning to get the cooking underway.

Faye was coming over to help in a while. Anthony hoped he could steal her away for a few and talk to her. He remembered her keeping vigil at the hospital. Faye never said anything to him about the incident since he awoke from the coma. He wanted to reassure her that all was well and that he didn't blame her at all. Anthony's physical therapy was coming along smoothly. He still experienced some stiffness after sitting for a long time and he couldn't eat as much as he used to. He'd lost close to twenty five pounds since the incident. He wasn't complaining though, he wanted to lose twenty anyway. He had tried the gym and Michelle bought rice cakes and baked everything she cooked trying to keep him on the straight and narrow. But he loved to cook and eat and often indulged in rich foods. Chelle was so good to him. She took care of him and the kids, the house and still fit work in. He couldn't wait for the doc to give him the thumbs up so that he could get back to work. He was starting to feel like a bum laying around the house doing nothing while his woman went to work.

Anthony channel surfed and finally settled on the sports channel. He had just settled in when the doorbell rang. "I'll get it baby" he yelled into the kitchen. He tried to situate himself so that he could get up out of the chair. Michelle came out of the kitchen wiping her hands on her apron. "Oh no you won't mister! You just sit down and rest yourself." Michelle put her hands on her hips to let him know she meant business. Anthony smiled at her sassiness. "I can see now I'm gonna have to tame that attitude you've got young lady" he teased. Anthony missed making love to his wife. He tried but she was so afraid they'd hurt something. He'd have to convince her tonight once and for all.

Michelle threw him a flirtatious look and went to the door. Faye had arrived with two handfuls of bags. "Faye, I told you that you only had to bring the drinks. What is all of this?" Michelle asked taking some of the bags so that Faye could hang up her coat. "Anthony and the kids love my banana pudding and I promised Michael that his auntie Faye would make him some. So there!" Faye said and tossed Michelle a look. Anthony heard them talking and threw in his two cents. "That's right baby. We love auntie Faye's banana pudding. I'm looking forward to a big bowl of it too." Anthony loved Faye's pudding. He had to fight the kids just to get some every time she fixed it. Faye came in to the family room and hugged and kissed Anthony while Michelle went back into the kitchen to give more orders to Alyssa. "Hey big guy, have you been takin' it easy?" She said sitting on the sofa. "I'm trying Faye. Chelle won't let me do anything." He said gesturing towards the kitchen. "I'm feeling fine. I think she wants to keep me here and all to herself." He said smiling. Michelle yelled from the kitchen. "I want you two to know that I can hear everything you're saying. Be careful Anthony…you know you still can't run very fast yet. I could do awful things to ya and no one would know." Anthony leaned over towards Faye. "Ya see what I mean Faye. The woman's gone mad!"

They laughed and Faye stood to go get started in the kitchen. "Well let me get in there before the Sergeant comes to get me." Faye

turned to leave and Anthony grabbed her hand. "Sit for a minute
Faye. Chelle and Alyssa can manage for a few more minutes." Faye
sat down and steadied herself. She knew this day would come, the
day when she'd have to hear how disappointed Anthony was in her.
She braced herself and looked him in the eye. She was ready for
this. It was time she faced her demons and her loved ones. She
wanted them to know that she was a new person. Anthony put the
TV on mute. "Faye, we've never really talked about what
happened." Faye wanted him to know that she didn't mean to put it
off. "Anthony I…." she started but Anthony interrupted her. She
looked at the carpet and got ready for what was to come. "Let me
finish and then you can say what you have to say." He lifted her
chin so that she could look at him. "In life, we all make some bad
decisions. Lord knows I have. The key is learning from those
decisions. For as long as I've know you Faye, you've been on the
giving end. You have a terrific heart and you will make a fine catch
for any man. You just have to filter out the knuckleheads."

Anthony thought for a moment and smiled in spite of himself. "Men
are natural predators. We can sense a woman with vulnerabilities.
Men use that to get what they want and Calvin was just another
piece of scum that sought you out." Taking some effort, Anthony
used his legs to make the recliner sit in an upright position. "What
I'm trying to say is, take some time to get to know who Faye is and
what Faye wants. When you meet a guy, don't accept anything less
than what you know your worth. You have a terrific support system.
We all love you and want nothing but the best for you. Michelle
showed me that true love can be had. She accepted my flaws and
helped me to improve because I had her to live for. I have her to
thank for everything that I am. That's what true love feels like. It's
not about having your heart torn out. You understand what I'm
saying right?" Faye had tears streaming down her face. Anthony
didn't blame her for what happened. He still had faith in her and
that meant the world to Faye. "You know I didn't tell you this but I
remember you coming to the hospital. Pauline said that you told her
that you were my sister." Faye wiped at her eyes and felt a little
embarrassed. She'd gone to the hospital and sat at his bedside. She
would talk for hours because she needed to feel like someone was
listening and not judging her. Anthony gave her an understanding

look. "I know that you blame yourself for what happened to me that night. I remember you telling me about us being the only family that you've got because you don't talk to your parents. You have to know that we're all here for you Faye. We are your family, all of us." With that he gave her a brotherly hug and Faye felt like a weight had been lifted. "Now, you'd better get in there before Alyssa messes up my banana pudding." Anthony laughed and Faye hugged him again. Faye thought to herself that this was her time. She would be making a lot of changes in the New Year.

Chapter 36
The Gospel Bird

Everyone arrived at three on the nose. Gayle and Erik brought the mac-n-cheese, Marie and Parnell brought the bread and desserts and Michelle's parents brought the greens and green beans. Michelle's dad made greens like no other. Michael hosted the UNO game while AJ showed his granddad, Erik and Parnell how to play Madden on the PlayStation 3. Alyssa was making her cooking debut and was busy with the ladies in the kitchen. She'd made the sweet potatoes and the potato salad with little coaching from Michelle. Since her dad's accident she'd been thinking on how to tell her parents about what Terrell had done. She was afraid that if she told them, they'd take her out of the recital and she would die if she didn't dance. She was a ball of nerves ever since he tried to come on to her. In the beginning, all of the girls thought he was cute, but she never thought to follow through with her infatuation. It was a harmless crush. That is, until he crossed the line.

Michelle finished setting the table and went to sit on the arm of Anthony's chair. He put his arm around her waist to make room for her. Michelle whispered in his ear. "That was very nice what you said to Faye baby. I'm sure she feels a lot better now that you all have talked." Michelle rubbed the top of his head and kissed him on the cheek. Anthony chuckled and whispered back to her. "You are so nosey baby. You were supposed to be in the kitchen concentrating on dinner. A man can't even have a little privacy in his own home." Michelle slapped him on the back of the head and they laughed. Anthony tightened his grip on her waist. "Actually, I was hoping you were listening. I've pulled out every trick I have to get you to agree to make love to me. I figured if you saw how compassionate I was, you'd give in." He looked around to make sure no one was listening. "So what do ya think, let Big Daddy show you what you been missing later on?" Michelle couldn't help but giggle. "I guess we can see if Big Daddy is fit enough to go a couple of rounds." She kissed him on the lips this time and he could feel her pressing her breasts against him. "Umph woman, don't start nothing now. We can have dinner upstairs if you keep this up." Anthony said with his bottom lip between his teeth. Michelle gave him a look to let him know it would be on later tonight. She got up from the chair and made the announcement that dinner would be ready in ten minutes.

The table was set beautifully with Michelle's finest China and flatware. She had to put the leaf in so that the table could easily fit twelve. She placed five on either side and she and Anthony at both ends. Michelle had an announcement to make during dinner. She and Anthony agreed that this was as good a time as any to tell everyone. Michelle's dad blessed the food. His blessings were always eloquent and heart felt. He'd been a deacon in their church for over twenty five years and she loved to hear him pray. After the blessing, it was family tradition for everyone to say what they were thankful for.

Anthony started. "This has been quite a year. I certainly have a lot to be thankful for. Let's see, I opened another office in downtown DC, my children are excelling in school, and I have *the* most wonderful wife in the world, hands down." Michelle blew him a kiss and the other men groaned. "On a more serious note though, I never thought I'd be thanking God for allowing me to come through the fight of my life just recently." He looked at Faye and then Michelle. "It's almost surreal how in your prayers you thank God for your life, health and strength but it becomes so routine that you forget it's meaning. So today I'm thankful for another chance to sit amongst my family and friends and to love them without condition." Smiles and applause was heard around the table.

"This brings us to our announcement" Michelle said standing. She made the walk to Anthony's end of the table and got down on both knees and took both of Anthony's hands in hers. "I want to profess my love to you in front of the people that we love most. I almost lost you just a few short weeks ago and I realized that you are truly

113

my souls mate. Will you do me the honor of becoming my
husband…again?" Anthony pulled her to her feet and onto his lap.
He kissed her and told her of course he'd marry her. He looked to
Michelle's father. "Dad, you think you could pitch in with this one
too?" Everyone at the table laughed and Michelle's dad said "I gave
her to you over fourteen years ago buddy. The bank is closed."
Michelle gave Anthony another sloppy kiss and took her seat.

Faye looked around at everyone and thought she may as well go
next. "I'm truly blessed to have friends that love me. I'd like to
thank all of you for standing by me." Michelle's mom put her arm
around Faye for added support. "I know I've made a mess of things
in the past but I've put some things in motion to prevent that in the
future. For the last month, I've been seeing a therapist that is
helping me to come to terms with my relationship with my parents
and with men. I've also spoken to one of the accountants at my firm
who's helping me with a plan to open a restaurant in downtown DC.
It will affectionately be called *Auntie Faye's* because Lyssie, AJ and
especially Michael have always been my number one fans of any
endeavor I've embarked on." Everyone looked around the table in
amazement. They all applauded her and everyone blew kisses and
expressed how glad they were for her. Faye had never been good at
keeping secrets. The kids seemed pleased that they were able to
hold it in. Apparently, they were the only ones that new about the
restaurant. Michael yelled out in excitement. "I told you I could
keep a secret AJ! I thought of the name, didn't I Auntie Faye?"
Michael couldn't keep still in his seat he was so excited. Michelle
sat at the end of the table and Michael was to her left and AJ sat
across from him to her right. She had to hold on to Michael so he
wouldn't fall out of his seat. Faye sat next to Michael and hugged
him. "You sure did baby." She said winking at AJ. "You sure did."
Last month, Faye put her office on notice. In four months she would
be leaving to open the restaurant.

Michelle was overwhelmed. "Faye that is fantastic news, I am so
very proud of you. That is quite a lot to be thankful for.
Gayle…Erik, I'm not sure if you can top that, but you guys are next.
"Erik and Gayle sat next to AJ and then there was Marie and Parnell
sitting next to them. Gayle cleared her throat and reached for Erik's

hand. "Anthony said it best, it has been quite a year. As you all know, Erik and I have had some issues this year." She looked at him and he squeezed her hand gently, encouraging her to go on. "Erik and I have decided to separate." Michelle, Marie and Faye all looked at each other and then at Gayle. They couldn't believe what she was saying. She'd never had the courage in the past to make Erik live up to his actions. This Thanksgiving was turning out to be the event of the year.

"This actually isn't a bad thing" Gayle said. "This is something that we've discussed at length. We are separating for six months to piece together our lives and to see if this marriage is where we want to be." Gayle started to tear up and she let go of Erik's hand to dab at her eyes with her napkin. Erik told them that he and Gayle still loved each other. He admitted to making a lot of mistakes and couldn't expect her to just accept them. They intended on going to counseling at the church separately and then together. Erik told them that he had a lot of issues that he needed to clear in his head before trying to commit to Gayle again. "So again guys, this is a good thing" he said. "We are going to work on ourselves individually so that we can be better for one another." With that he kissed Gayle and there wasn't a dry eye at the table. After everyone gave their input on what they were most thankful for, the eating commenced. Everyone praised Alyssa's sweet potatoes. They all agreed that she'd make an excellent cook someday.

Chapter 37
The Virtue of Patience

Alyssa sat and watched everyone give their testaments and looked over at her dad who seemed enthralled in it all. She knew that eventually she'd have to tell them what happened at the studio with Terrell. She had never kept anything from her parents and didn't want to start now. The recital was in two weeks and she wanted them to know what was going on in case he tried something else. Everyone looked so happy now though and she didn't want to spoil things. She new she had to tell them sooner rather than later.

A good time was had by all and contrary to popular belief, Michelle's stuffing was spectacular. Even Anthony had to comment on how delicious everything was. He told Michelle that he'd start on the dishes while everyone had dessert. She tried to protest but Anthony wasn't having it.

Michelle packed take home plates and Alyssa ran her dad out of the kitchen and put everything away and helped her mom clean the last of the dishes. Anthony saw their guests to the door and retired to his recliner in the family room. AJ and Michael were upstairs in their respective rooms and Alyssa saw this as an opportunity to talk to her parents. She sat at the table in the kitchen and motioned for Michelle to join her. She told her mom that she's always felt that she could talk to them about anything that was bothering her. Michelle agreed and paid closer attention realizing that this conversation was more serious than she thought. Alyssa told her that some things had been happening at the dance studio that was starting to bother her a little. Alyssa was actually trying to feel her way and read Michelle's face to see if it was alright to go ahead. Michelle reassured her and told her that she could always talk to them about whatever was going on and they'd always try to be as fair as possible.

Alyssa told her about the incident with Terrell and how he'd been pitting the other girls against her. She told Michelle that he'd been pressuring her to allow his advances or she'd never be able to dance professionally without him backing her. Alyssa felt sick every time her parents dropped her off to practice. Terrell would rub against her when he walked by or chose her when he wanted to show the girls a new position. He'd stand behind her and whisper awful things to her. When Anthony was in the hospital, the last thing she wanted to do was cause more worry so she kept it to herself. Michelle sat in utter disbelief. "Lyssie, it's our job to take care of our children. I don't care what's going on, if there is a matter with our children that takes precedence over everything else." She got up and stood next to Alyssa and hugged her tight. "I'm so sorry baby. I had a feeling that there was something about Terrell but I had no idea it was to this extent." She looked Alyssa in the eye. "I saw the instant message conversation that you all were having. That wasn't Angie that you were talking to was it?" Michelle waited for her to respond. Alyssa looked down to avoid her mother's eyes.

Michelle lifted her chin so that Alyssa could look her in the eye. Alyssa finally let the tears go. "Mom, I didn't mean to lie to you. It's just.....well, all of the girls kinda had a crush on Terrell. We thought it was so cool that he'd traveled the world and worked with all kinds of famous people." She wiped her face with the back of her hand. "When he complimented me and seemed to single me out..." she hunched her shoulders. Michelle finished for her. "You were flattered right? You thought you could really go far if Terrell was in your corner right?" Michelle gave her a gentle smile. Alyssa hugged her mom around her waste. "I've really made a mess of things haven't I mom. I'm so sorry I didn't tell you and dad." She looked up in horror. "Dad is going to hate me when we tell him. He'll be so disappointed in me. Mom please can you tell him for me?" She stood and wiped her face once more. She looked over her shoulder to make sure no one was listening. "Please mom. Dad can never stay mad with you." Michelle took a napkin and wiped the tears from her oldest child's eyes. "How about both you and I go in

and talk to daddy. He's really a big push over…especially for you."
Alyssa looked reassured and she breathed a huge sigh of relief. Her
dad was the last person that she wanted to let down. Since she was
the oldest and the only girl, Anthony had always spoiled her.

Anthony had dosed off and the TV was watching him. Michelle and
a nervous Alyssa walked in to the family room. Alyssa posted
herself on the couch across from Anthony and Michelle went over
and shook him. It took a minute but Anthony finally woke up to find
his two favorite ladies looking at him. "See this is what happens
when you won't let me do anything. I'm forced to take naps and veg
out in front of the boob tube." Michelle smiled but Anthony could
tell that this wasn't a social call. Something was up with these two.
"Whatever it is, I didn't do it." He said trying to make light of
things." Michelle moved over closer to Alyssa. "Baby, Alyssa and I
need to talk to you." Anthony sat up and turned off the television.
"Well, I'm waiting." Anthony said looking directly at Alyssa.
Alyssa leaned in to her mom until there was no space separating
them. Her dad had a way of looking at her that made her want to run
and hide. She picked at her pink nail polish and tried to find the
right place to start.

Alyssa decided to start from the beginning. Anthony sat there the
entire twenty minutes never saying a word. He fumed on the inside
but put on a neutral face. He didn't want Alyssa to be afraid to tell
him everything. Apparently Terrell had been antagonizing her ever
since she refused him. He couldn't believe this had gone on for over
a month and a half and this was the first he was hearing of it. After
she finished he got up and went to sit next to her sandwiching her
between he and Michelle. He put his arm around her and kissed the
top of her head. "Lyssie, this should never happen again. Your
daddy is always here for you no matter how bad the situation may
be. You understand me?" Alyssa got out a yes daddy before he
continued. "Now I'm not gonna lie. I'm a little hurt that you didn't
tell your momma and I about this before now but I'm proud of you
for telling us. Terrell needs to know that it's not OK to treat young
ladies like this and I intend to tell him." Alyssa lifted her head and
looked at her dad. "Daddy please don't do anything to him. You're
still healing and I don't want you to get in any trouble. Besides I

still want to dance." Anthony gave her a nudge and smiled at her. "Lyssie I wasn't born yesterday. Your daddy still has a few tricks up his sleeve. Do you have any idea how many police officers and guys not so close to the law I grew up with?" He pulled her close to him again. He looked over and winked at Michelle. "Don't you worry sweetheart. That little punk won't be doing this to somebody else's baby, I can guarantee that."

Chapter 38
Change will Come

Gayle sat in her office and tried to focus on the project that was due to her client this afternoon. Even though she and Erik had their differences, it was hard to sleep at night without him. He'd been at his new apartment for almost two weeks now and she had to admit she missed him. Erik admitted to having an affair with Pamela and a few others throughout the course of their marriage. She wasn't sure what compelled her to want to stay with him. She'd definitely had enough of the lies and the games though. Something had to change. Her sanity depended on it. After trying to concentrate for the past two hours she finally decided to leave early and surprise Erik with a packed lunch at his office. Their counselor suggested they start dating each other again. This would help them to get to know each other again. Maybe it would bring back the spark that they once had.

Erik was serious this time. He loved Gayle and wanted their marriage to work. He told the owner of the company that Pamela would have to be assigned to another design team. He and his boss were friends and he told him the truth about Pamela not being good for his marriage. Today was her first day with another team on another floor. He certainly couldn't have her fired so this would have to do for now. He sat in his office going over the plans for the new strip mall in Upper Marlboro, Maryland. There was a knock on his office door and Pamela didn't wait to be invited in. Erik looked up at her. He took off his reading glasses and moved things around on his desk to avoid eye contact. "Pamela, hello" he said. "Cut the bull Erik" she said walking towards his desk with her hands on her hips. "What the hell is going on? First you call me last night and tell me that we can't see each other and then I come in and I'm on another team?" She leaned across his desk so that he had no other option but to look her in the eye. "You need to be explaining to me what this is all about Erik, before I get angry." With that she sat in the chair in front of his desk. Erik massaged his temples and let out an exasperated sigh. He told her that he'd come clean with Gayle and they were going to make their marriage work. He apologized to Pamela and told her that he thought it'd be best if she were assigned to another team to avoid conflict. "Well gee thank you very much for being so considerate of me" she said sarcastically. She wanted to know what caused the sudden change of heart. Just last week they were in bed together and today he was professing his love for his wife.

Erik went around to the other side of his desk and sat in the chair next to Pamela. "Listen, I know I'm totally at fault here Pamela. I have to make some changes in my life. I love my wife and I need to see if we can make this thing work out between us." He looked down at the floor and realized that Pamela wasn't going away without a fight. He looked at her again and told her that he needed to get back to work. She could not believe he was talking to her as if they'd met yesterday. She reached over and grabbed his face in her hands. "Listen Erik, I know I rushed you. I'm sorry about that. You don't want to be with her, you said so yourself. You said that she wasn't stable. You have to give us a chance Erik, please." She covered her face with her hands and started crying. Erik felt like crap. *Lord please help me out a little here.* He took her hands in his and told her that he'd been lying the entire time. Gayle hadn't done anything to make him stray. He was just a selfish bastard that took advantage of the opportunity. Pamela snatched tissues from the box on Erik's desk. She looked him in the eye and finally realized he was serious. Her intent was never to hurt Gayle. Erik was such a ladies man. He seemed to be a good catch and she was ready to settle down. She had to give it to him though. If he wanted to make things work between he and his wife, she certainly didn't want to begrudge another woman. She stood and got herself together. "I appreciate what you're trying to do Erik." He stood also and gave her a reassuring smile. They walked around the seating area towards the door. "Well, I guess this is it, huh." Pamela said. They looked awkwardly at each other and in an attempt to show him that she understood, she reached out and embraced him in a hug. He hugged her back and was grateful that this didn't get ugly.

Gayle walked past the receptionist area and figured that the receptionist was probably at lunch. She switched the lunch basket that she'd rushed home to pack in the other hand and walked towards Erik's office. She ran her hand across her hair and looked down at herself to make sure her skirt wasn't twisted and then opened the door to Erik's office. Gayle thought she'd fall out right there on the spot. The basket dropped to the floor and Gayle stood there in total shock. "What the......" was all she could get out. A startled Erik and Pamela turned to see Gayle standing there. Erik was the first to respond. "Baby, it's not what you think. I was just explaining to Pam..." that was all he could get out before Gayle slapped him with such force that he was momentarily dazed. Pamela took a few steps back in fear that she was next. "Don't you dare try to tell me why I just saw my husband locked in an embrace with another woman?" Gayle walked back and forth with her hands balled into fists. She couldn't believe she was willing to give him another chance.

Erik recovered and walked over to Gayle trying to calm her. "Gayle, listen. I was telling Pamela that we were going to make things work." He looked over to Pamela for a little help. Pamela was still a little afraid. She cleared her throat in an attempt to get the words out. "Gayle, Erik is right. I was just leaving. The hug was just a goodbye hug. Really, it meant nothing." She started to walk towards Gayle but when Gayle looked at her she thought better of it. Gayle felt exhausted all of a sudden. She didn't give it a second thought. "My lawyer will be in touch with you Erik. Make this your last time speaking directly to me." With that she picked up the basket and threw it at his head. Erik ducked and the basket just missed him. Sandwiches and cold slaw splattered on the side of his desk. Gayle straightened her suit and pulled her coat back up on her shoulders and took her exit.

Erik turned to go after her. "Gayle, please wait baby. You don't understand." He followed her to the elevators not caring about the people openly staring at them. Gayle felt physically sick and couldn't even look at Erik. Gayle stared straight ahead refusing to even acknowledge Erik's presence. She pressed the elevator button again and again. *What the hell is taking the elevator so long?* He was making a bigger fool of himself running behind her yelling and carrying on. Erik knew better than to push Gayle at this point. She wouldn't even look at him. "Gayle, if you'll just give me one minute baby, I can explain this. I've changed Gayle. I promise." She couldn't believe he was pulling this crap. Finally the elevator arrived. She walked in and turned around and jabbed at the door close button until finally the doors obeyed. As the doors closed, Erik stuck his leg in to stop them from shutting.

All of the secretaries watched in amazement. Usually Erik was so polished and laid back. They couldn't believe he was putting himself out there like this. He had tears running down his face and cold slaw dripping from his shirt. "I love you Gayle." He said desperately. "I know I've been an asshole in the past but I've changed." He said. Gayle looked around a little embarrassed. Erik could care less about who heard him. He couldn't lose her. He continued to hold the doors open until the alarm sounded. He mustered up the courage and took Gayle's hand and gently pulled her off of the elevator. "Please Gayle. Nothing happened baby, I promise." Pamela walked slowly out of his office. Erik was a disheveled mess and she couldn't believe he was begging.

Gayle went reluctantly but didn't want to hear any more of his excuses. "Erik please...not here." Erik stood in front of her and said, "Gayle you have to understand, I was just telling her that we were making things work." He grabbed her shoulders to stop her from walking. "I know you can't trust me right now. But please...please Gayle, you have to know that I don't love anybody but you." Erik was crying openly now. Gayle reached up and wiped his tears. If he was lying, he was doing one hell of a job of it. One of the secretaries yelled out, *girl, go on and give him another chance.* Gayle looked around at the crowd that had gathered and then back at Erik. He wrapped his arm around her shoulders and she finally relented. They held each other and everyone in the office clapped and ahhhed. Erik took her by the hand and they went back into his office. As they passed Pamela, Gayle gave her a look that said she could forget about any more late night rendezvous with her husband.

Chapter 39
My Mister Wonderful

Parnell sat back in the corner of the couch to give Marie more room to stretch out. She rested her head in his lap and they watched Mr. Wonderful...again. This was one of Marie's favorite movies. When it was released in 1993, she thought maybe she still had a chance at love. Years later accompanied by a trail of failed relationships, she was happy she'd finally found her Mr. Wonderful. Parnell was the most patient man she'd ever met. He taught her to let down her guard a little and allow someone else to take the reins in the relationship. They were looking at the part where Gus went to Leonora's apartment and strung lights throughout the courtyard and remembered all of the names of the various plants that she'd planted there in hopes of winning her back when the phone rang. Marie jumped up and ran into the hall to answer, cursing herself for missing her favorite part. She picked up on the fourth ring. "Hello" she said in a sing song voice. "Marie, how've you been?" John said hesitantly. Marie almost dropped the phone as she looked over to make sure Parnell was still watching the movie. "Hhhello. Uh...I'm fine. Umm...How are you?" Marie couldn't believe that John had called her.

She hadn't talked to him since he called her an ice princess and a shell of a woman. She'd never forget that. Parnell glanced over at her and she smiled and put up a finger letting him know that she'd be a minute. "Hold on a minute please." She tried to sound as professional as possible. She told Parnell that she needed to take this upstairs. He told her to hurry. She almost broke her neck running up the stairs. She went into her bedroom and closed the door. She tried to catch her breath before picking up the phone. "John, what do I owe the pleasure of this phone call?" She couldn't understand why she was so nervous. "I was wondering if you could have lunch with me this Friday. I thought maybe we'd go to Georgia Brown's. I know that's your favorite." He said. There was an uncomfortable pause before he went on. "I need to speak to you, and I'd like it to be in person." Marie paced her room wondering what the hell he wanted to speak to her about. I mean it had been almost three years since they last spoke. "Look John. I'm not sure I'll be able to meet you. Is there something specific that can't be said over the phone?" Marie went to her door and cracked it open. Satisfied that Parnell was still watching TV, she turned back to the conversation. "I just need to see you, is that all right Marie? I promise not to take up too much of your time. Just say you'll meet with me, please." Marie was actually a little curious as to why he wanted to see her. They agreed to meet at two. Marie sat on the bed for a minute to ponder the phone call when Parnell called from downstairs. Marie got up to go back downstairs. Whatever it was that John wanted, she had three whole days to wait and see.

Chapter 40
Fanning the Flame

Marie walked into the restaurant and looked around for John. She made sure that she didn't wear anything too revealing yet leaving something to the imagination. She wanted him to know that she still had it going on. He waved her over from a table by the window. Marie walked gracefully over to the table and took the seat across from John. Always the gentleman, he stood until she had taken her seat. He leaned over and kissed her on the cheek. "Marie, It's good to see you." They smiled at each other and exchanged pleasantries. Marie felt like she was somehow betraying Parnell. She told him that she couldn't have lunch with him because she was meeting a client. Why had she lied to him? She tried to focus so that hopefully she could get this over with as quickly as possible. "John, what's with the urgency? Is everything all right?" She said this in an effort to get him to spit out what he wanted. He thanked her for meeting him and told her to relax and enjoy her meal. He'd taken the liberty of ordering her favorite, stuffed pork chops, and the waiter had just brought the food to the table. Marie couldn't believe he remembered. She promised that she wouldn't finish them both and she'd do an extra thirty minutes on the treadmill tonight.

John couldn't help but notice that Marie seemed more at ease and not as uptight as she used to be. Even the way that she dressed wasn't as stiff and business as usual. They ate their meal and had light conversation. Finally just after they ordered coffee, John got to the reason he'd asked her to meet him. He started by apologizing for the way things ended with them. He was angry and had tried to hurt her. He told her that he'd thought of her often and wanted to call but didn't have the courage. Marie tried to keep her facial expressions as blank as possible. She never told anyone that she couldn't eat for the first week after they broke things off. She followed his career even to date and she was proud of his accomplishments. But that was all behind them now. "John is there something that you need to say? I mean...I truly appreciate your acceptance of your part and I too am sorry for how things ended but that was a long time ago." Marie said.

John took his napkin out of his lap and looked at Marie pensively. "I've been thinking about you a lot lately Marie. I know this is a bit awkward but we were very good together. I'd like to give us another try. I mean...I don't know if you're dating someone or not and I certainly don't want to interfere. I just can't help but think that we should give it another shot." Marie took a moment to register what he was saying. "John I... I don't know what to say." *What the hell was going on here? I haven't heard a peep from this man and now after almost three years he wants things to go back to what once was?* John sat and waited for a reply. Marie couldn't help but think back to when they were together. They had the same goals and they were both very driven. Somehow their careers became more important than each other. Marie felt very warm all of a sudden. "John, I am dating someone right now. What brought this on? Listen, we haven't spoken to each other in almost three years and now you just spring this on me." John put his hand to her mouth the stop her. "I understand Marie. Is this guy that you're seeing serious? I mean, are you in love with him?" Marie could not believe what was happening. "John..." Marie felt like she needed to leave.

She felt like she was backed against a wall or something. "I...I do love him John. He's very good to me." There, she said it. She never really told anyone the way she felt about Parnell other than her girls. It felt oddly liberating. John didn't seem fazed at all. "Marie we compliment each other. We are go getters, and let's face it we were a powerhouse couple." He leaned back in his chair. "Are you telling me that you don't believe that?" Marie admitted that their ambitions are what brought them together in the first place. But there was no question that Parnell loved her and she loved him. She'd just come to terms with all of her control issues and they were having a ball loving each other. "John, thanks so much for asking me to come and I'm happy that we can be friends. But I am in love

John, and I can't entertain the thought of jeopardizing that." Marie started to gather her things and he got up to help her with her coat. "Think about what I've said Marie. Things are really happening for me right now and I need you more than ever." He sat back down and Marie turned to go. John took a sip of his coffee and took out his credit card to pay the bill. "You know how to reach me Marie. Give me a call when you decide that you still love me." He said assuredly. With that Marie left and was thankful for the chill outside. This couldn't be happening. She dug in her purse to find her cell phone. She needed to hear Parnell's voice.

Chapter 41
The Shindig

Michelle looked in the mirror putting the finishing touches on her makeup. She sat at the vanity in her bra and panties because she didn't want to wrinkle her gown. Her parents should be arriving any minute to watch the kids. Anthony came and stood behind her and wrapped his arms around her. She nuzzled her head against his chest and took in the smell of his cologne. He kissed her cheek and ran his hands in between her thighs. "Mrs. Moore, I'd like to thank you for this morning *and* this afternoon for that matter. Your performance was exemplary I must say!" Michelle smiled at him through the mirror. She playfully smacked at his hand so that she could finish getting ready. "Why thank you sir. Anytime you need my assistance, please let me know. I'd be more than happy to oblige." She shushed him away and he went back into their walk in closet to pull out his tux. Their good friend was being honored by the fire department for rescuing a mother and child from an apartment fire a few months ago. The fire and police departments held an annual ceremony for outstanding service and they always attended along with Marie, Faye and Gayle. Anthony had grown up with several police officers and fireman so they were always on the invitation list. Anthony thought how funny it was that he and Michelle grew up so close to each other and even knew a lot of the same people but had never met. He was happy his friend had convinced him to try the food in the carry out in her neighborhood. Otherwise he would've missed out.

Michelle's parents finally arrived and they and the children sat and waited in the family room for Michelle and Anthony to make their grand entrance. Michelle yelled down that they'd be ready in five minutes. This was the first time that they'd gone out since Anthony's accident and Michelle wanted it to be special. The ladies had gone shopping and Michelle brought a gown that would knock Anthony's socks off. He got dressed in AJ's room and she locked herself in their bedroom. She yelled out to him to see if he was ready. After perfecting his bow tie, Anthony waited in the hallway for Michelle. He had on an Armani tux with his spit shined gators adding the finishing touch. His man at the barber shop edged him up nicely and he thought he looked pretty sharp for an old man. Finally Michelle opened the door and Anthony had to do a double take. Michelle had on a Vera Wang black form fitting gown that had him drooling. The gown had a plunging neckline with a tie at the empire waist. It shimmered with beaded trim details and had Godet styling at the bottom. Anthony could not take his eyes off of her. "Somebody better call the law cause you gonna cause a disturbance up in here!" He said. Michelle blushed and took his hand so they could walk downstairs together.

Michelle told him that she'd have to keep an eye on him tonight. He looked sharp as a tack and she didn't want the ladies to *even* get the idea that he was there unescorted. When they got downstairs the kids whooped and hollered. Alyssa said that they looked like they were going to the prom. AJ gave his dad some dap and told him he looked cool. Michael went over and took Michelle's hand. "You look like a princess mommy." He said looking at her dress shimmering. Michelle bent down and gave him a peck on the forehead. "Thank you sweetheart! Now you stay here and make sure AJ and Alyssa follow the rules. You have to help Grandma and Grandpa out OK?" Michael nodded and ran over and jumped in his Granddad's lap. Michelle winked at her parents and told Anthony to get a move on.

Chapter 42
Playing it Safe

All in attendance was dressed to the nines. The event was held in a restored mansion in Frederick, Maryland. Anthony and Michelle waited outside for the others to arrive. It felt so good to get dressed up and have a evening with friends. Anthony said his hello's to some of the officers and firefighters as they entered. Michelle couldn't believe how many people he knew. Anthony got a lot of business by word of mouth. Since his trailers hauled basically anything, he always got good business from the local owners and had contracts with government agencies. Parnell and Marie pulled up first and then Gayle and Erik with Faye in tow were the last to arrive.

The ballroom was elegantly decorated in platinum and black. The grand chandeliers glistened and each table was lit by candlelight. The ladies went to claim a table while the men checked their coats. Marie was able to find a table that was near the dance floor but not too close to the band. As they took their perspective seats Marie noticed that John and his date was seated three tables over from them. Marie cursed under her breath and made it a point to seat with her back to them. *What the hell is he doing here,* she thought. *This can't be happening to me.* Faye and Michelle noticed John at the same time. Faye slid into the seat that was for Parnell. "Did you notice that John is here tonight?" Faye looked in his direction and Marie yanked her arm so that she jerked back around. Faye winced in pain because Marie was digging her nails in her hand. "Ouch! Can you please let go of my hand you maniac!" Faye said. Marie slowly let go of her hand and whispered sorry to Faye. Gayle had come back to the table with a ticket from the bar for the bottle of wine that she ordered for the table. She looked at the others and took her seat asking what she'd missed. Michelle filled her in and

Marie but on her best act looking uninterested. Michelle said, "You know he knows a lot of the guys on the police force Marie. He's also very involved in the children's programs that the police have put in place. It's only natural that they'd invite him this year." Marie rolled her eyes at Michelle. "I know that Michelle." Marie said taking a sip from her water glass. "I just don't feel like dealing with him tonight." The ladies couldn't figure out why Marie was so bothered by John's presence. Last they'd heard Marie hadn't spoken to him since their breakup. It was clear that Marie hadn't come clean with something.

Marie straightened her back and looked straight ahead as she noticed the men making their way to the table and took their seats. Anthony took his seat in between Michelle and Faye and whispered in Michelle's ear. "There isn't a woman here tonight that looks as beautiful as you do." She leaned into him and put her hand in his lap. "Awww...baby, thank you. I did this to impress you ya know?" She said. Anthony kissed her on the cheek. "You could've worn a potato sack and some Chuck Taylor sneakers and they still couldn't hold a candle to ya!" he said. Marie scowled at them. "Hello...get a room why don't you. There are other people sitting at the table ya know." Parnell took her hand and wondered what the change in her mood was all of a sudden. Anthony and Michelle laughed at Marie as one of the bartenders brought over their wine.

The band started playing Frankie Beverly's *Before I Let Go,* and people started making their way to the dance floor. One of the police officers that Michelle grew up with made his way to the table. Reggie had known Michelle since grade school when she used to beat him up at lunchtime. He was an attractive man now and clearly had eyes for Faye. He said his hello's to everyone at the table and looked in Faye's direction. He complimented her on how beautiful she looked and asked if she'd like to dance. Faye looked like a deer caught in headlights. She looked at Michelle and Gayle and then back at the guy. "Thanks, but I'm going to sit this one out." She said. He told her that was the only pass she got and he'd be back later to ask her again. The guys lead their dates to the dance floor and Faye stayed behind with the excuse that she'd watch the purses.

On the dance floor, Anthony told Michelle that he saw Reggie at the coat check and gave him permission to ask Faye to dance. Anthony thought it would help get her mind off of her troubles so that she could have a good time. Reggie's niece danced with Alyssa and Anthony didn't tell Michelle that he'd also informed him of what Terrell had done. That was all that needed to be said. Reggie promised that it wouldn't happen again. He spun Michelle around and put his hand around her waist. Michelle was a great dancer and Anthony was proud to have her on his arm.

Michelle noticed that Gayle and Erik seemed so in to each other. It was almost like they'd just started dating. After the song was over they walked hand in hand back to the table as Anthony and Michelle decided to stay and dance to the Luther ballad that the band started to play.

Marie laid her head on Parnell's shoulder and finally began to relax. She hadn't made eye contact with John since the evening started and planned to keep it that way. She and Parnell had made arrangements to stay at a nearby hotel for the weekend and she didn't want her mood to ruin that. All of a sudden Parnell stopped dancing. Marie looked up to find John tapping him on the shoulder asking to cut in. Parnell nodded OK, winked at Marie and went back to their table. Reluctantly, Marie took John's hand and they started to dance. "What do you want John?" She whispered through clinched teeth. "This little stunt isn't funny at all." She said looking around. "Where is your date anyway?" John smiled at her and twirled her around. He told her that he just wanted a dance, that's all. "Why are you so uncomfortable Marie? Have you given any thought to what we talked about?" he said. Marie stopped dancing and snatched her hand away. "There is nothing to think about John. Please, let's just leave it at that!" Marie stormed off in the direction of the ladies room. Michelle told Anthony that she was going to check on her. Gayle and Faye followed up the rear.

Parnell was about to follow also when both Anthony and Erik told him to hold tight. Erik shook his head at Parnell. "Trust us man, you don't even want to go out there right now." Anthony slapped him on the back and said, "Have a glass of wine with us and just chill. Let the ladies work this one out." Parnell hunched his shoulders and sat back down. He asked them who was the guy that Marie was dancing with. Anthony explained that they used to date a few years back and that they didn't part as friends. Parnell relaxed and made small talk with them but wondered if he should've gone after Marie.

The ladies followed pursuit to see about their friend. Marie sat in a stall and hugged her shoulders. Gayle knocked on the stall door. "Marie, what is going on? What did John say to upset you so much?" Faye grabbed her handkerchief out of her purse and passed it over the stall door to Marie. Michelle coaxed her out of the stall. Marie came out blowing her nose. She went over to the mirror to fix her makeup while the ladies waited for her to fill them in. They all went to the seating area in the bathroom and sat down. Marie explained to them that she'd met John for lunch and that he'd been calling her ever since wanting to get back with her. In one of their conversations he mentioned that it would be great for his image. Not that he loved or missed her but that he was on the fast track and needed the right woman to complete the package.

She told them that the lunch was pleasant enough but then the phone calls started. He told her since she didn't really want to be with a man that she could just reap the benefits of his up and coming success. Since she was an entrepreneur and he knew a lot of people, if he decided to run for office it would be great for both of them. "That smug little bastard!" Gayle said. "What gives him the right to treat you like a commodity rather than a person with feelings?!" Marie laughed in spite of herself. "You know what's so funny, yall? A few short months ago I may have taken him up on his offer." She wiped her face and washed her hands as her friends stared in disbelief. She tossed the paper towels in the trash and headed for the door. "Let's face it. I haven't been coined as a very likeable person, have I?" She said. "It hurts a little that he called me on it." She said. They all gathered around her. Michelle hugged her around her shoulders and said, "You are a changed person Marie. We've all noticed it. You've met your match in Parnell. You guys are great together." Michelle shook her a little and smiled at her in hopes of raising her spirits. Gayle took her hand and said, "Chelle's right Marie. To hell with John with his condescending ass! He's just

135

jealous because he also sees the change, *and* he's envious of that fine man you have sitting out there." Other ladies came into the bathroom and they all gathered themselves, did one last check in the mirror and made their way out of the ladies room.

John was standing at the entrance of the ballroom. Marie told them to go on in and that she'd be right behind them. They all gave John wicked looks as they walked pass him. He walked across the lobby to Marie and stood in front of her. "Is everything alright Marie? Your cohorts aren't too happy with me. Was it something I said?" He was so coy she couldn't stand it. "Look John. I'm not the same person I once was. I'm finally happy and I don't need you trying to interfere." She started to walk away when he grabbed her by the arm. Other people took notice of the obvious. He whispered in her ear. "Look Marie, I'm sure this little fling with the book writer won't last long once you start being yourself. I know for a fact that you haven't dated anyone since we broke up. Do yourself a favor and tell Mr. Suave to go on back to New York so that you and I can pick up where we left off." Marie snatched away from him and picked up the front of her gown so that she wouldn't trip hurrying away from him. Before she stormed off she stated matter-of-factly, "Don't flatter yourself John. Parnell is his name and he is more of a man than your cowardly ass ever was. Like I said, don't call me anymore. I'm not interested in being in a superficial relationship with you or anyone else. I happen to be in love with him. Oh…I'm sorry, you wouldn't know anything about that."

She threw her head back and turned to go back into the ballroom with him on her heals. He reached her just as she was about to go inside. "You owe me you bitch!" Marie tried to ignore him and kept going. She almost knocked Parnell down as he was on his way to see about her. She looked flustered for a moment and tried to regain her composure. Parnell grabbed her hand and turned her to face John. He'd heard the latter part of their conversation and was happy that Marie and publicly acknowledged her love for him. Parnell extended his free hand to John. John looked Parnell up and down before deciding to shake his hand. Parnell's grip was a little firmer than necessary. "I don't think we've had the pleasure of meeting. I'm Parnell, the one who will kick your natural ass if you ever speak to this woman that way again." They dropped hands and John looked smugly at them both. Parnell turned to Marie and slid his arm around her waist. "Now, if you'll excuse us, my lady and I didn't get a chance to finish our dance." Marie smiled up at him. They turned and made their way back to the dance floor. John was left to pick his face up from the floor.

A great evening was had by all. Faye even danced once or twice with Reggie. Gayle and Erik elected to get a room at the same hotel as Marie and Parnell. Anthony and Michelle told them that they needed to get home to relieve her parents. They had promised to sit with the kids at least once or twice a month to give them some time together. Although she was certain her parents wouldn't mind, she didn't want to impose too long.

Chapter 43
Plié, Sauté - Dance girl, Dance

Alyssa and her company were putting on Swan Lake and she was the lead. Alyssa had practiced dance since she was five years old. She expressed an interest when Anthony and Michelle took her to New York to see the Nutcracker. Since then she'd done everything from tap to modern dance to her love, ballet. Her body was and ideal dancers body. She used her long legs to do some of the most beautiful *Jeté* (leaps) and *Fouetté* (a turn or spin on one leg) that her instructors had ever seen. She definitely had the talent to become a professional dancer.

All of the dancers had to be at the playhouse a couple of hours early for one last practice before the show opened. Anthony voiced his concerns about leaving her there without him being there. Since Alyssa told him what had been happening, he made it his business to sit in on the rehearsals. Since he still had a week or so before he returned to work full time, he made sure Alyssa wasn't out of his sight unnecessarily. All of the instructors had been at the last three rehearsals to help them master their runs and give them pointers on how to improve. Terrell really didn't have an opportunity to get to her during that time.

He did corner her coming out of the bathroom before the recital. He told her that he didn't care that her punk ass daddy was there. Alyssa tried to move around him and he blocked her path. "Let me know when you're ready to stop playing hard to get." He moved even closer to her and licked the side of her face. "I'll have you calling *me* daddy when I'm through with you." He snickered as he walked away. Alyssa thought she'd die on the spot. She felt physically ill and was tempted to tell her parents that she didn't want to perform. She went back into the bathroom and scrubbed her face.

She looked at her self in the mirror and took a long hard look at herself. After a few minutes of contemplation, she decided she wouldn't give Terrell the satisfaction of stomping on her dreams. A few of the other girls told her that Terrell had tried to turn them against her but they knew that the things he said weren't true. He'd even attempted to make advances towards them. Alyssa decided at that moment that this would be the end of it.

Alyssa took center stage. She stood in fifth position and waited for the curtain to be raised. She was dressed in white from head to toe. Her long hair was tightly pulled back in a bun. Her tutu was a pale pink and she had on pink diamond studded earrings that her grandma had given her. Her tiara sparkled with pink and clear rhinestones. Alyssa was shaking like a leaf. This certainly wasn't her first performance but there'd be recruiters there from several schools as well as her family and friends. She wanted to do well. Next year she'd be starting high school and she wanted to go to a performing arts high school. This was it....the director gave her the countdown and the music started. *Please lord,* she prayed. *Help me out here. I need to clear my head and nail this not only for my family and friends, but to show Terrell that he hasn't broken my spirit. Amen.*

Anthony sat on the end of the row with his video recorder ready. The girls had been practicing for months to get to this performance and his baby was the lead. Michelle sat beside him trying to quiet Michael and AJ. Their entire row was filled with grandparents, Gayle and Erik, Marie and Parnell, and Faye had even allowed Reggie to escort her tonight. Alyssa's first instructor had even cleared her schedule to come and support her. The lights were dimmed and the curtain slowly rose.

Anthony did his homework about the ballet. *It was about a prince that had come of age and was having a birthday celebration. All of the girls were after him but he didn't pay them any mind. His mom gave him his gift and told him it was time for him to marry. Not wanting to accept the responsibility, he goes off in the woods to hunt with his friends. He comes to a lake where he finds a beautiful swan called Odette, the Swan Queen, played by Lyssie.* Alyssa came out of position and the audience was quieted. She commanded the stage with her grace and beauty. The guy who played the prince sat there looking like he was really entranced by her. Alyssa was so light on her feet that she seemed to float across the stage. She smiled the entire time and managed to glance in the audience to catch her dad with his camera. Her performance was superb and Anthony couldn't remember anyone else's performance in the entire ballet. At the end, the audience was on their feet. The cast took their final bow and then they parted and Alyssa walked through taking her bow. Anthony and Michelle couldn't contain their excitement. Michael and AJ whooped it up for her. Anthony noticed that Alyssa was so overjoyed that she had tears in her eyes.

Before the last curtain, Reggie excused himself to go to the men's room. He and Anthony exchanged a look and nothing else needed to be said. Reggie did some checking with the NYPD and found out that Terrell had fled the city after three teens from a performing arts school accused him of fondling them. He was scheduled to appear in court a month ago but never showed. Tonight he'd face the consequences. Everyone waited for Alyssa to changed and join them. When she walked through the door from backstage AJ and Michael were the first to get to her. AJ had flowers that he bought with his own money and Michael had a gift that he and Michelle had picked out special. Alyssa hugged them and said, "You guys can be really sweet when you're not driving me crazy." She kissed AJ on the cheek and picked Michael up. "OK runt. What's in the box?" She said. Michael told her that it was a secret and she had to open it up. "Alyssa put him down and opened the small box wrapped in pretty pink paper. She opened to find a silver necklace. Ballerina slippers hung from it with two small diamonds in the middle of each. Alyssa was at a loss for words. Finally she said, "This is the most beautiful necklace that I've ever seen." She kissed Michael and he grinned from ear to ear. By this time everyone else had made their way over to them. Everyone told Alyssa that she did a wonderful job. Anthony hugged her tight and told her that he was overwhelmed with pride. "You were absolutely magnificent baby." She laid her head on his chest and knew everything would be alright.

Chapter 44
Curtain Call

Reggie did in fact go to the rest room. Afterwards he made his way
back stage. He flashed his badge and asked the director where he
could find Terrell. He found him in the dressing room going through
the girls' things. Reggie proceeded to treat Terrell like he was
resisting arrest with a few extra punches for good measure. Terrell
cried like a girl and wanted to know who the hell he was. Reggie
had him pinned to the floor face down. He flashed his badge and
said, "I'm a cop you little pervert. You like messing with little girls
huh?" He grabbed Terrell by the collar of his shirt and pulled him to
his feet. "I'm going to make sure I tell the guys in holding that you
enjoy that type of thing. They have something special for little
freaks like you." Reggie led him out in front of the production staff,
the dancers and the audience members that had lagged behind.
Everyone including Alyssa got a chance to see Terrell squealing as
Reggie practically carried him out. Anthony held Alyssa closer and
told her, "I told you not to sleep on your daddy, didn't I? Terrell
won't be bothering you or anyone else anytime soon." He took her
hand and signaled to all the others. "Now let's go and get something
to eat, my treat!" he said winking at Alyssa. "We need to celebrate
my little girl's big night." While everyone else wondered why
Reggie was locking up Terrell, the Moore family breathed a sigh of
relief.

Chapter 45
He is Faithful

Auntie Faye's opened the first Saturday in April. Michelle decorated the restaurant in shades of reds, greens, and browns. She read somewhere that these colors are popular food colors and that red is often used in restaurant decorating schemes because it is an appetite stimulant. They'd worked for the last two months with decorators and interviewing staff and chefs. Faye had been prepared to open the doors two weeks ago but saved the grand opening for today. Anthony and Michelle's ceremony was today and the reception would be held there. It was a simple gathering of close friends and family. Michelle was dressed in a simple but beautiful spring dress that accentuated her curves. There were small delicate flowers in her upswept hair. Anthony wore a eggshell white linen suite with a lavender shirt to compliment the colors in Michelle's dress. Michael was the ring bearer and was dressed to kill in a suit like his dad's. AJ, also in white linen, had brushed up on his piano lessons so that he could serenade his parents as Alyssa did an expressive dance. There may have been maybe sixty people in attendance and the weather had obeyed and was perfect to say the least.

Faye was only able to stay until after they'd finished reciting their vows before she had to sneak out to get back to the restaurant. Even though she had a top notch staff, *she* needed to be there to make sure everything was to her liking. Reggie had left with her to help her prepare. Faye liked him but made it very clear that she was in the midst of getting to know herself and needed time before she would even think about a relationship. Reggie proved to be diligent and stayed the course, waiting for the day that she'd see that he was serious about her.

Everyone seemed to arrive at the same time. The crowd gathered outside of the restaurant until Anthony and Michelle were front and center. There was a huge bow on the door of the restaurant and various bundles of spring colored balloons placed on either side of the entry way. The sign that read *Auntie* Faye's swayed slightly with the warm breeze. Faye stood at the door and waited for the crowd to quiet down. "I'd like to first congratulate my dear friends on their renewed commitment to one another. I'd also like to acknowledge all of my girls that have stuck by me during this transition. Join me in christening a new establishment, a new life and a new embarking of what I hope to be a long lasting one." Gayle, Michelle and Marie stood hand in hand as Faye took scissors and cut the bow. Everyone applauded and the four friends shed tears of joy as the crowd made their way into the restaurant. Faye had arranged for tables to be cleared to make a small dance floor in the center of the restaurant. Michelle and Anthony took their first dance. Afterwards couples made their way to the dance floor. Faye stood off to the side nodding her head. *Thank you Lord for hearing my prayers. You are truly faithful and true to your word. I love you and I finally understand.*

And steadfast is the Lord, who shall establish you, and shall guard you from evil. *2 Thessalonians 3:3*

Made in the USA
Lexington, KY
30 March 2014